CHANGING PERCEPTIONS ONE GUIDED STEP AT A TIME!

CHANGING PERCEPTIONS
One Guided Step at a Time!

JANICE WHITTLE

ISBN: 978-0-6455527-1-3

Published by Janice Whittle
Front & Back Covers – Designed by Janice Whittle

First Printing, June 2024

DEDICATION

This book is dedicated to all the past, present and future Guide Dogs that undergo intense training to improve the lives of people with vision impairment but yet experience so much unacceptable discrimination.

CHANGING PERCEPTIONS

One Guided Step at a Time

Janice Whittle

&

Keegan the Guide Dog

All Paws on the Floor

My name is Keegan, and I'm a Guide Dog,
Not just a pet bought through a catalogue.

It cost over $50,000 and 2 years to train me,
To guide Mum around because she can't see.

My rights are protected by law,
So please welcome us through the front door.

In the restaurant, I guide Mum to a table,
And just pray that the chair is stable.

I'll be quiet and lay under her chair,
Customers won't even know I'm there.

As she dines, I will just sleep or chill,
Then guide her to the counter to pay the bill.

She thanks staff for the wonderful service as we leave,
Then I wonder what adventure she has up her sleeve.

Mum orders a taxi so we can get to our next destination,
It's such a relief when the driver greets us
without hesitation.

I ask you to respect the discrimination law,
Nothing less, nothing more.

You can always ask for identification,
And Mum will put you at ease with clarification.

I'm a Guide Dog and protected by law,
I keep all paws on the floor.

*"Real change, enduring change,
happens one step at a time."*
Ruth Bader Ginsberg

FOREWORD

I first met Janice Whittle while catching up with her then-partner, Bob, a mate of mine from our Army days.

I was immediately struck by her unique and intriguing individuality. Her sense of fairness and justice are also admirable qualities, and her sense of adventure is always inspiring to those of us who are fortunate to know her.

Having volunteered for Guide Dogs Australia as a puppy raiser for thirteen years, I know from first-hand experience that a Guide Dog is meant to give its handler the freedom and confidence to step into a world that was previously not so easily accessible.

Keegan and Janice are a perfect match. Keegan is a highly skilled Guide Dog who has been trained to assist Janice with everyday living. He helps her navigate busy streets, avoid obstacles, and keep her safe. They have experienced many wonderful adventures together.

However, what has surprised me are the challenges that having a Guide Dog has added to Janice's already difficult life. Between the pages of this book, we are taken on a journey that sees a visually impaired handler (Janice) learning life's lessons about discrimination the hard way.

The attitudes she has encountered are enough to have made anyone quit and give up on their dreams of being able to live a 'normal' life just as any sighted individual might do. Instead, Janice has said enough is enough. She has found her voice and together with Keegan is using it to break down barriers that should not exist.

This book will make you laugh, make you cry and most importantly, make you think about what we often take for granted. It will educate and inspire you to make your voice heard when you witness an injustice.

It is all about changing perceptions one guided step at a time. Guided by the experiences of Janice, guided by Keegan to lead the way so the world becomes a better place for those living with a guide dog.

In this inspiring, much needed book, Janice and Keegan lift the curtain on discrimination as they share the story of their 3 years together, of what it means to persevere by following a pathway that has enabled them to raise awareness of both conscious and unconscious bias within our community.

With admiration and respect.

Eddie Stone
March 2024

Becoming a Guide Dog

At 8 weeks old, I moved in with Helen, the superhero who started my journey towards becoming a Guide Dog.

"I candidly call them the blank canvas," Helen said when asked about raising puppies. I'm their first influencer, and it's lovely. It's scary because it's my responsibility to do a great job."

"I love it when they first come home, and I am building that connection with the puppy. When Keegan first arrived, we had already scheduled a trip to Mount Glorious with visiting friends. My husband and I carried him around the National Park. He wasn't fully vaccinated, so he could not be put down, particularly in a National Park, as they wouldn't be happy either."

"We carted him around the park, and he really connected with us. I think that helped him feel safe. They're very much like human babies. They want to feel loved and connected."

As a young pup, I soaked up every lesson like a sponge. I grew more confident and skilled each day as Helen lavished me with praise, saying, "What a cuddly, beautiful boy you are". She made me feel ready to take on the world, and my joy was expressed by wagging my tail happily. I loved being able to please, and most of all, I loved the way Helen made me feel special.

As the months passed, there was always something new to learn. Helen's patience and guidance were invaluable on this journey. She taught me the basics as she showered me with love, teaching me how to be a loyal friend and a source of comfort in times of need. Cuddle time was the best, but Helen never allowed me onto the furniture beside her.

Helen taught me to walk on a loose leash; I had to stay by her heel and not pull on the leash. That was tough as I often wanted to walk faster than she did. I mean, I have four legs, and she only has two, so it made sense that I should go faster - that was not allowed!

"You need to be obedient, Keegan", she'd stroke and praise me whenever I did well. I quickly learnt to obey and, before long, could sit, go down on command, stay, and stand - I loved the treats she gave me for following instructions!

Each day, we walked. Sometimes to different places where I had many new things to sniff and experience.

When I was 8 months old, it was time to leave Helen. I moved houses, where I moved up to advanced lessons, exploring different areas. There were lots of new experiences to enjoy and places to explore. It was a fun time learning all these new things!

When I was 14 months old, I became a bed and breakfast boarder. My handlers would drop me off to classes five mornings a week at Guide Dogs Queensland and pick me up after lessons. Here, I was taught the final skills: navigating busy streets full of traffic, avoiding obstacles, finding objects, and learning new commands that would keep my future human handler safe.

I heard people talking about how a Guide Dog was expensive to train and that not all dogs made the grade. I had to pass an exam to become Keegan, the Guide Dog.

I wondered what the difference was between me and other dogs, but as time went by, I learnt that the role of a Guide Dog is to help make life easier by guiding someone with low vision. I was important. Someone with low or no vision would, with my help, be able to get out into the community instead of being confined to the four walls of their own home.

Time flew as I went through my training drills. Some of the basic tasks I had to master were stopping at curbs, walking in a straight line, avoiding obstacles, stopping for traffic, and finding an empty chair. The most difficult challenge was walking past the meat counter in the supermarkets, and all those bags of carrots piled right at my nose level were another hurdle. Did I tell you how much I love my carrots? I'm proud to say I passed the tests.

Our family must be pretty smart, fast learners. I say this because my sisters, Kacie, Kelsea, Kensi, Katie, Kleo, Kahlia, and I all graduated as Guide Dogs. Yep, I'm the only boy in the family. You might have noticed that all our names begin with the same letter of the alphabet; that's because each litter of puppies is named alphabetically.

I can tell you if you're wondering where I got my name. It's cool, really. The people who sponsored me got to choose my name. Fun fact: sponsors are the people who pay for us Guide Dogs to go through all the intensive training that we need to actually do our jobs. It's a hefty sum of money to invest in a dog that is going to someone else, so these sponsors are definitely wonderfully community-minded and seriously generous.

It takes over two years and costs more than AUD$50,000 to raise, train and transform puppies into Guide Dogs. Now, back to my name…it was quite an honour to learn that I am named after the son of my sponsor – he's a pretty handsome dude, too.

Graduating, as I discovered, was a memorable experience where I got to be all dressed up (just like humans who graduate). "He looks so handsome." Cameras and mobile phones clicked and flashed as I did my best poses. I even became the poster boy for Guide Dogs Queensland - a proud moment for my puppy raiser and trainers. "Yes, Keegan, you did good!"

Helen, who raised me as a puppy, came to my graduation. After getting permission from my new Mum, she even made me a rather fancy mortarboard for the occasion. I am wearing it on the front cover photo of this book.

Just like humans have licences, passports, and other sorts of identity documents, I have papers identifying me as fully trained and skilled in looking after my designated human. You only get these papers if you successfully graduate. These papers also come with a card for my human, as they must also be trained. Not everyone can have a Guide Dog. There is a strict application process and a waiting list. We are matched up as a perfect pair to work together. I had no clue what kind of a human would be deemed a good match for me. I just knew it was going to be someone special.

After graduating, I officially became a working Guide Dog; I knew I was ready to fulfil my purpose. Guiding and assisting would be my mission in life. With my head held high and my tail wagging furiously, I was ready to make a difference, one guided step at a time.

*"Silence is the last thing the world
will ever hear from me."*

Marlee Matlin

Hotels & Motels

Bribie Island is situated not too far from where I live. Having booked and paid in advance for two nights' accommodation before Keegan and I had paired, I wanted to do the right thing; excitedly, I contacted the accommodation I'd booked to inform them, as a courtesy, that I'd be bringing my Guide Dog.

I was looking forward to spending time by the water, feeling the sand between my toes, the water lapping at my ankles, and the sun on my face—although I do have to be mindful of slipping, slopping, and slapping on the sunscreen, given that I am a natural redhead. With Keegan as my Guide Dog, I would be able to take full advantage of the lovely walking pathways on Bribie.

Less than 10 minutes later, my mobile phone rang. It was a lady from the booking office.

"We have cancelled your booking." When I asked why, the response was, "We don't allow dogs at our resort."

Despite my efforts to explain that a Guide Dog was legally allowed and the fact that it is against the law to refuse a Guide Dog, her determined response was, "No, we are exempt from those laws."

The argument continued for several minutes but to no avail. They were adamant that the booking was cancelled. I was not to show up. There would be no room for me. To say I was taken aback by the blatant discrimination I was facing is an understatement. It was disheartening to see the level of determination to keep me away; to make matters worse, they refused to refund my money. Wow! Talk about turning the tables. According to them, it was my fault because I was unlawfully going to bring a Guide Dog.

Through all the training Keegan and I underwent together, there had never been any mention of refusal of entry. I have since discovered that refusals are common. There are some exceptions to where Keegan cannot go, which are all detailed in the Act; they include procedural areas of a health service, ambulance, and food preparation areas.

The Act states that anyone in control of a public place, public passenger vehicle or place of accommodation can be fined for refusing entry, refusing to provide service, or imposing a term that would separate myself and Keegan.

In shock, reeling from the incident and feeling incensed, I decided that I would not accept being refused entry when the law of Australia was on my side. The Guide, Hearing and Assistance Dogs Act 2009 (the Act) came into effect on 1 July 2009.

Under the Act, handler(s) and their certified dog have access rights to public places (such as restaurants and shops), public passenger vehicles (such as trains or taxis used to transport members of the public), and places of accommodation (such as hotels and campgrounds).

The definition of place of accommodation under the Act is consistent with the definition of accommodation in the Anti-Discrimination Act 1991 and includes:

* a house or flat

* a hotel or motel

* a boarding house or hostel

* a caravan or caravan site

* a manufactured home under the Manufactured Homes (Residential Parks) Act 2003

* a site within the meaning of the Manufactured Homes (Residential Parks) Act 2003

* a camping site.

My fighting Irish spirit had been stirred, and the flames of righteousness were burning bright. I took the decisive step of lodging a complaint with the Human Rights Commission (HRC).

Since lodging that case, I have learnt that it takes what seems like forever for anything to happen once the complaint is lodged. The wait can be as long as 12 months, which is probably why many business owners gain that false sense of security that there will be no repercussions.

The role of the commission is to get both sides of the story and to help resolve the complaint if appropriate. A letter is sent advising that a complaint has been made against that business or person. Once the letter arrives, the first step is to try for conciliation by helping both sides talk and hopefully negotiate an agreement.

There are three main things that I am looking for when I attend conciliations:

1. A genuine apology rather than simply lip service.
2. Make changes to policy and procedures so no one else goes through the same experience.
3. All staff are to undergo training so they are aware of the law.

Lastly, we will talk about money.

Regarding my Bribie Island accommodation, the property owner refused to refund me, citing that I had not turned up for my booked dates. Mediation did not resolve the situation, with the owner trying every trick in the book to avoid giving back my money. His behaviour made it abundantly clear he was prejudiced, biased, and judgemental. Without having ever met me, he was basing his perceptions on a stereotype he had of someone with a disability.

He mentioned that I had booked a double bed instead of a twin and that, as an unmarried woman, I would be sharing a bed with someone out of wedlock. It was none of his business, and it could not have been further from the truth. The reason I had booked a double was that it was actually cheaper than a twin.

The next argument cited was booking without telling them that I was in a wheelchair and needed to be on the ground floor. It was news to me that I was in a wheelchair!

When he announced that I couldn't even walk more than 100 metres, I burst out that I was doing a 5k run. Oh my God, I heard everything from him. There was no way that we could come to an agreement in mediation. All I wanted was my money back. I didn't want compensation for stress and trauma, although by then, I would have been entitled to it. It was insulting and affronting that I should be pigeonholed based on his stereotyping.

Despite the challenges with the property owner, I stayed hopeful and determined to find a resolution. I contacted Blind Citizens Australia for help, providing them with all the necessary documentation and evidence of my booking. With their support, and after a protracted negotiation I finally got the $780 dollars that I had paid for my accommodation. There was no apology, and the owner remained adamant that they had been in the right to refuse Keegan.

Not long after the incident on Bribie Island, and before my case with HRC had even come to conciliation, I was booked to travel to New South Wales. My trip was to Casino, a small country town in the hinterland on the North Coast of NSW.

All arrangements had been made before Keegan came into my life. The accommodation had been pre-booked and paid for in full as it's my habit to pre-book and lock in a rate so I know exactly what my expenses will be for each trip. Once again, I gave them the courtesy of messaging to advise that I'd be bringing my Guide Dog; there was no response to my message. Deciding there was nothing to be lost, I apprehensively rocked up with Keegan in his Guide Dog harness.

Two ladies at the front desk looked up as we walked in. One said, "We got your notice that you're bringing your Guide Dog with you, so we've made changes to your booking."

"Here we go," flashed through my mind as visions of more arguments danced in my head.

The other lady chimed in, "We want to make sure your stay with us is as comfortable and enjoyable as possible."

"We've made the changes because you only booked a small room. We've given you a free upgrade. So, you have more space for your Guide Dog." You could have knocked me over with a feather!

I shook my head to ensure my ears were not playing tricks on me. The smiling faces of the reception staff assured me I had definitely heard correctly. Unable to contain the grin spreading from one side of my face to the other I thanked these wonderful ladies. They assured me they were willing and available to assist with anything I needed during our stay. Their warmth and hospitality made me feel genuinely welcome.

How totally different were the two receptions I'd received less than a month apart? Both reservations were made before Keegan came into my life. Both properties were notified on the same day, but the contrast in treatment was strikingly different, poles apart.

The friendly, hospitable welcome reminded me that sometimes the best adventures can be found in the most unexpected places. The lovely welcome by staff at the River Park Motor Inn in Casino made me feel more at ease about travelling with Keegan.

The warm reception enormously boosted my wavering confidence; up until that point, I was apprehensive and haunted by visions of us being refused accommodation everywhere we travelled.

Another standout positive experience was staying at the Hotel Allen, Townsville. I first visited there in February 2022; Keegan and I had no trouble, and again, a lovely warm welcome was extended to both of us. What makes this hotel exceptional was my second visit in May 2022.

"Welcome back, Keegan & Janice", greeted us as we entered the reception. They even had a little gift of treats for both Keegan and me.

I don't need gifts; I just want to be accepted like anyone else and allowed in. Don't get me wrong; it was such a delightful surprise as I am more used to being refused entry and experiencing abuse.

I've chosen to participate in every parkrun in Australia, which means completing runs in over 500 areas. Naturally, that involves different and often more out-of-the-way locations, and each of these locations requires overnight accommodation. It's sad that when I go places, it is always in the back of my mind, wondering if I will be given a hard time with Keegan.

Planning the different runs is a highlight of my life, as this is the one place I feel genuinely welcome. Dogs are allowed, and a Guide Dog is respected. No one disturbs Keegan when he is guiding me on my runs. The parkrun each Saturday allows me to explore new places. Being told I would never be able to walk again is what has given me the drive to do all the parkrun challenges.

My medals include 5km, 10km, 12km, 21km, and 130km. In March 2024, I completed my first-ever half marathon. I'm happy to say I did 21.1km and over 28,000 steps. In August 2024 I will participate in a 200km Running Against Violence event. Not bad for a blind epileptic; just remember you are the creator of your own destiny.

When Keegan is on duty, he is calm and focused. Put him on the leash, and he's a well-trained dog. Off leash, Keegan is boisterous and loves to run, roll around on the grass or in the sand, and generally zoom around the place.

It's a testament to the excellent training that Guide Dogs undergo that Keegan is able to easily switch into working duty mode the moment I put him in his harness. He loves his work and that's obviously because he never puts up an argument about wearing the harness.

At parkruns, I will always take the time to explain to the children what it means to be a Guide Dog, what his harness means and why they cannot touch or talk to him when he is working.

The kids are like little sponges. I hear the sparks of curiosity and eagerness in their voices as they listen intently and ask questions; I welcome their questions. It is heartwarming to see understanding begin to dawn and I find it encouraging as I believe it is through education that attitudes and perceptions towards Guide Dogs and those with disabilities will be changed.

The small interactions the parkrun children have with Keegan are hopefully sowing the seeds to shape a more inclusive next generation that understands discrimination is wrong. Although the laws exist to protect us and allow Guide Dogs access, education is lacking, resulting in the myriad of discrimination that Keegan and I experience on an all-too-regular basis.

####

Going to Weipa in August 2021 for the Fishing Classic meant I needed a flight and accommodation. The now somewhat familiar record of refusal began to play out once the accommodation realised Keegan was coming with me. They insisted that I take up the matter with Qantas, with whom I had booked both my flights and accommodation. Eventually, when I could prove Keegan was a Guide Dog with all the necessary paperwork, the accommodation very reluctantly agreed we could stay.

I lodged a complaint with the HRC before heading for Weipa. On arrival, we were made to feel distinctly unwelcome and that we were being accommodated under duress. They were having us there because they had been told they had to.

When the case finally came to mediation, the owner, who appeared genuine, stated that in all the twenty-plus years that he had owned the premises, it was the first time he was aware that Guide Dogs were permitted and that to deny access was against the law.

He immediately offered me an apology as soon as he realised they were in the wrong, and I accepted this as it was sincerely meant. He also, of his own accord, offered monetary compensation to make amends for the shabby treatment and discomfort I endured at his property. When he asked how much I wanted, I suggested that he give me what he felt was fair. I am not in the business of seeking to make money from lodging complaints. For me, it is about creating change and ensuring that the discrimination stops.

####

One of the worst cases of discrimination I experienced was on June 2nd, 2023 when I visited Toowoomba. I'd booked one night of accommodation at the National Hotel using Booking.com because I knew the location from when I had previously lived in the area; staying somewhere I was familiar with would make it easier for me to get around. I received my confirmation and receipt as I had paid in advance.

My friend drove me to Toowoomba, as we were both going to participate in Picnic Point Parklands parkrun the following morning. We arrived at the National Hotel at 4:20 p.m. I got out of the car, and Keegan guided me into the hotel and to the bar, where I was handed a form to fill in and my booking confirmed. Danielle, who was serving me, and I shared a little giggle about general things as I completed the form before being handed my room keys.

As Keegan and I followed, my friend walked ahead searching for Room 6. Placing our bags on the two double beds. I got Keegan's water bowl out of his Guide Dog backpack and planned to go to the communal bathroom to fill it with water.

As I turned around, Danielle approached the room and told me to 'pack my bags and leave'. I asked her why and she said, "We don't allow pets".

I explained that Keegan, who was still in his official harness, is a registered Guide Dog. She could clearly see that he was still in uniform.

"We don't allow service dogs either" was her response. She'd apparently been sent up by management and told to instruct me to leave immediately.

Instinctively reaching for my phone, which I'd popped down on the dresser inside the door when we entered the room, I pressed it to record mode. The video recording commenced at 4:39 p.m. It was less than 19 minutes since we had arrived outside the hotel.

"So Danielle from National Hotel in Toowoomba, you are saying because I have a service animal, I am being kicked out of the National Hotel which I have paid for."

"You can request a refund; you didn't say you had a service animal; if you did, we would have refunded it before," came back her retort.

"Under the laws, I do not have to, I have paperwork with me that states that he is legally allowed in here."

"You also have to ask the place you're staying at," responded Danielle.

"No, I do not." The argument continued back and forth.

Things got uglier when I asked for the manager, "I don't have to tell you that." The receptionist continually refused to accept that a Guide Dog was legally allowed. She was on a high with power and not prepared to listen to anything I had to say. "I will call the police," said Danielle.

I refused to leave, stating that I would stay until they arrived.

At 4:44 pm I posted a photo of Keegan lying beside a bed in the room with his harness on my Facebook page "Janice's Vision of Life" so my followers could see another refusal of service we were experiencing.

Feeling seriously shaken, I desperately rang around to find other accommodation for the night. As I frantically dialled numbers, I could hear my heartbeat reverberating in my ears; it was pounding so fiercely I felt it might burst out of my chest. Furiously tapping the buttons on my phone, it crossed my mind to wonder if this chest pain was what a heart attack felt like. I didn't have time to think properly, my brain was more scrambled than usual and finding a place to stay was my priority.

I had put on a brave face, refusing to leave, but there was no way I could stay where I was. The Wilsonton Hotel, another venue where I had previously stayed on several occasions, was fully booked.

Danielle returned to our room with a mobile phone in hand; a female (who I am guessing was the manager) was on the other end. She told me that she had rung the Police Link to have me charged and arrested for entering the hotel with a service dog. I could hear the female on the phone telling Danielle to instruct me to leave. Danielle left when I told her again that I would wait for the police.

She came back again a few minutes later, telling me that I could stay the night because I had paid, even though I was breaking the law by having a service dog in the hotel without permission.

By this time, I had thankfully found an alternate place to stay, so I informed her that I would be leaving, picked up my bags, and made my way to the bar. I asked for a refund. The response was that I would have to apply for a refund through Booking.com. Bob returned the keys, and we left.

My chest pains began to ease as we pulled up at The Coachman Motel, which thankfully had a vacancy. When we arrived, I flipped my phone to record mode before leaving the car; I was ready for any trouble! The doors to the motel reception were locked, which made perfect sense as it was already dark. As I knocked, an Indian gentleman came forward to unlock the door.

"Oh, you have a Guide Dog!"

"Do you have a problem with that?" I asked in a somewhat terse tone. Internally, I was thinking, "Here we go again!" I experienced a flashback to the week before when I had struggled to get home after a trip because an Indian taxi driver had point-blank refused to transport Keegan and me home from Brisbane Airport.

"Of course not! He's a Guide Dog!" I could hear the smile in his voice as he unlocked the door gesturing for us to come inside.

Here I was in a hotel with an Indian male receptionist making me welcome. Yet, a white Australian female had thrown me out less than an hour previously from another establishment. The irony was not lost on me. Too often, we judge and make assumptions based on skin colour or ethnic background.

As he handed me the room key with a warm smile, I couldn't help but feel a sense of guilt for almost falling into the same trap of prejudice. I had almost made that same mistake myself in prejudging the reaction I would receive from this lovely gentleman.

Thinking about my experience, I realised how important it is to constantly be vigilant in challenging our own biases and preconceptions. Everyone has a unique story; none of us are cardboard cutouts, and that is what makes us human. It is crucial to allow everyone to show their true selves. We need to live in a world where diversity is our strength and for that to happen we need to all be able to embrace and celebrate our differences.

After checking into the room, we decided to go out for dinner as it was getting late, but before we headed out, I put in a request for a full refund with Booking.com.

In the meantime, one of my social media followers contacted me and recommended that I share the video footage of the unacceptable experience at the National Hotel.

Still feeling extremely agitated and stressed by my experience of being thrown out, I took her advice and shared the video of my refusal on social media. This video was uploaded at 5:53 p.m. The post went viral, reaching an audience as far away as the USA. Accusations that I was rude for recording what happened flew across social media, including that I was a professional who made a living out of suing people. To that accusation, my response is that my action of recording results from my experience of not being believed. Video evidence cannot be questioned.

As we drove to the restaurant for dinner, I contacted Police Link to give them my side of the story as I was worried. I didn't feel I should be arrested when I had not broken the law. I am wary, but not afraid, of the police as my experiences have not been positive in the past; in NSW when I was trying to escape my abusive husband, they were, for the most part, unhelpful.

The call with Police Link lasted 35 minutes. First, I spoke to Jess. After I told her that I was wrongly removed from the hotel, she asked if I had somewhere to stay for the night. Jess checked the legislation and informed me that service dogs are allowed in the hotel, and they have broken the law.

"Well, I know that, but they seem to think that I am the one breaking the law, not them."

I was then put through to Jessica, who also asked if I had organised other accommodation for the night. Jessica advised she would put a report through to the police, and they would get statements and press any charges necessary. She gave me the Police Link reference number.

Jessica took down my current accommodation details and my schedule for the next day. I would be heading back to Brisbane the following morning after I complete the parkrun. After getting off the phone with Police Link and finishing my dinner, I saw that I had received a message via my Facebook page.

The message was sent at 6:05 p.m., and went as follows:
"Hi Janice,

My name is Grant Wheeler. I am writing to you on behalf of the National Hotel. Please give me a call on 0402 xxx xxx Thanks"

At 7:18 p.m., I responded, *"What is your connection to the hotel?"* Grant Wheeler read my message immediately but did not respond. We made our way back to Coachman's Motel and went to bed.

On Saturday morning, June 3rd, 2023, I attended Picnic Point Parklands parkrun and, as is my habit, went to a café for breakfast afterwards. Whilst I was there, I received a call at 8:46 a.m. from SGT Goodwin from Toowoomba Police Station informing me that the police would not get involved in my complaint for two separate reasons.

"Number 1, we don't get involved with someone with a disability and secondly, we have real crimes to attend to". The call lasted 46 seconds. It was a very blunt refusal of service. To say I was shocked was an understatement, but at the same time, it was not entirely unexpected as I had been let down by police before. I felt so let down as I was again being treated as if I was the one who broke the law, yet I was entirely within my legal rights.

At 2:20 p.m. on Saturday afternoon, Grant Wheeler had sent another message.

"Dear Janice, The National Hotel would like to make the following statement with regards to an incident that occurred at the venue on Friday 2nd June. Our staff member was not made aware at the

time of check-in that there was an animal that would accompanying you during your stay. We naturally have a no animal policy in place at the venue. Upon seeing the dog with you and your guest our staff member enforcing the hotels policy of no animals in the venue approached you and informed you off our policy and that unfortunately in this situation you wouldn't be able to reside with us for the night. She informed you that a full refund would be issued and that she could help with other places to stay. After this interaction took place is when the video that you have shared started. Our staff member requests numerous times during the video to no be filmed and she states our company's policy. After leaving the upstairs area the staff member raises this issue with senior management and is informed that In this instance the staff member has made a mistake and under QLD laws guide dogs & legally registered support dogs are allowed to resides with their owners during their stay in paid accommodation. Upon realising that the young staff member has made a mistake she issued yourself with an apology and informs you that you are welcome to stay at the venue. You refuse to do so which is completely understandable and there is no issue with the hotel and we will provide a full refund when we receive the request from the booking agent you booked through.

We'd like to take this opportunity to again apologise for the mistake made by our young staff member. All of our team has been briefed on this issue and moving forward this won't happen again. We'd would like to add that we do believe that there is a much better way of handling these situations then to use social media and create a scene and situation that doesn't need to be created. This *entire situation could've and should've been handled in a much more professional and courteous manner than it has been. We don't believe it's fair that this young staff member has been ridiculed and threatened by other members of the public and has had to involve police for her own safety and well-being. Those actions have happened because of social media and whilst you are free to do what you'd like we don't believe that it is okay for this young staff member who made a mistake and then realised her mistake and apologised for it shoood be treated this way. We do genuinely hope you found somewhere to stay and we hope that in future this doesn't continue to happen to you or anyone else again. We would also like to ask that the threats and abuse toward this young staff member who made a mistake stops as it is not warranted and not appropriate. The hotel will be making no further comment on this situation moving forward. Regards Hotel Management"*

At 3:00 p.m. I responded. *"Several statements you made presented as fact are in fact not true. I will be taking this further with GHAAD and Human Rights Commission. I attempted to settle it immediately by producing GHAAD identification, but she refused to view it and said "pack your bags and leave". She continuously said the manager is demanding we leave and she was on the phone with the manager at that time. She also threatened to call the police and have me charged and removed. When she returned to the room the second time, she was asked if the police had been called, and she stated that she had made a report through Police Link saying it is a requirement of her job to do so. The only reason I called the police that evening was to explain the reason for her report and asked if the police would like my statement and to view the video. There was never an apology offered, nor did she offer to organise other accommodation. She did under protest advise that the manager said, since I have paid for the room, I can stay. At that point, I had already arranged other accommodation and decided I would not stay at a hotel that blatantly breached the law. On arrival at the hotel, I had my guide dog with me, so there was never any deceit on my part. As per your statement, I will be making no further comment. Regards, Janice and Keegan"*

My follower, Danielle, contacted the media, and I was then contacted by Channel 9, 7, 10, and ABC. The ABC took a different approach to the other channels. They asked for proof of identification to ensure Keegan was a registered Guide Dog. Once I had provided satisfactory identification that they could authenticate, the ABC also ran with the story.

A flurry of reactions and commentary exploded across social media as soon as the story aired across the 4 channels. There were two camps; those who wanted to condemn me and those who stood up against the discrimination I experienced.

The messages of support help make up for the awful, abusive, downright nasty and vicious comments that also flooded my social media page. One such message came from Muller Bros, who reached out to say Keegan and I would be welcome at their establishment, which dates back to the early 1900s, at any time.

On 6th June, I officially lodged a complaint with the Human Rights Commission against the National Hotel, Toowoomba, under the Disability Discrimination Act 1992 and a complaint with Queensland Government Guide, Hearing, Assistance Dogs under the Guide, Hearing and Assistance Dogs Act 2009. It's such a pity that basic rights are taken away from people with a disability and have to be settled through other avenues.

"What a load of shite" is the reaction when I simply share a story. Evidence cannot be disputed. Learning the hard way that I need evidence of what happened is why I now record on my phone.

Thomas Hughes contacted me on 22 June at 10.36 am and introduced himself as the new owner of the National Hotel, Toowoomba. During our 18-minute conversation, he stated I was his top priority job for the day. He explained he had seen me on television news regarding the discrimination. He suggested we start from scratch as he wanted to disassociate from the previous owners; he did not want to be blamed for their actions. He went so far as to give me their names and full contact details, including telephone numbers.

I suggested to him that I would be willing to assess the hotel based on my personal experience if he could provide me with accommodation and a meal at their bistro. However, he responded by saying that the place was going to be refurbished and that there would be no accommodation or bistro available for at least 12 months. Nonetheless, he did arrange to have my money refunded.

Interestingly, on 14 July, less than three weeks after our conversation, there was a Facebook post advertising accommodation available from 20 July. It does not take much to conclude that I was not welcome. I would go so far as to say that I was blatantly lied to. Although the hotel's name has been changed to The Nash, I noted on the Facebook post of 10 April 2024 that Danielle still works at the hotel.

I am fortunate to always have supporters who jump into the conversation, citing the legal rights of a Guide Dog. One of the biggest challenges is the growing presence of what I call "fake" assistance dogs.

A Guide Dog falls under the category of an assistance dog. Any assistance dog has a vital role to play and is a vital part of its handler. It could be its eyes, ears, etc. The dog is part of the human handler rather than having a separate identity. An assistance dog is not a pet.

Not all assistance dogs wear an identification uniform, but this does not remove the legal right to ask for identification to ensure it is a true assistance dog rather than a fake one. It is both legal and acceptable to politely request identification from a legitimate handler who has been trained with their service animal and knows to always carry identification with them.

A genuine handler will never take offence at respectfully being asked for identification because we are taught that identification helps maintain integrity. This also prevents misunderstandings or conflicts. Communication and understanding are key when it comes to interacting with assistance animals and their handlers. In Australia, the official term is an assistance dog, but many do use the term service dog, which is what is used in the USA.

One of the questions that will often pop up on social media, where I am extremely active, is about the difference between an assistance dog and a companion or therapy dog. That's a great question!

Assistance dogs provide assistance to individuals with disabilities (mobility, sight, hearing, and other physical and/or psychiatric issues). Unlike a Guide Dog, these animals do not need to pass an extremely strict Public Access Test (PAT). In order to pass the PAT test, a Guide Dog has to undergo intensive training; not all dogs have the right temperament to be able to be successfully trained to the high standards demanded of Guide Dogs.

Therapy Dogs have an important but totally different role. They do not have public access rights, but they do need to have basic good manners and be well-trained to respond to commands like sit, drop, heel, come, etc. These dogs are used as visitors to hospitals, nursing homes, and rehabilitation facilities, providing valuable therapeutic interactions. The dog should also meet the minimum standards of an Assistance Dog when out in the public arena and this means they remain calm and maintain appropriate social behaviour in a diverse range of environments. These dogs are usually also taught the skills to interact with people with various disabilities.

"With my Guide Dog by my side, I am empowered."
Janice Whittle

Meeting My Handler

Our humans are called "handlers" - go figure! I call mine Mum, but officially, she is my handler.

Being paired with my human was a special moment. I first met Mum when she came to Guide Dogs Queensland in Bald Hills. The powers that be had decided we were a potential match. It's not a random allocation. Personalities, energy levels, and lifestyles are all considered as part of the matching process. I had boundless energy and my new handler loved to go on parkruns, but we had to be trained together to see if we were a suitable match. I know this because I have heard my Mum explain this several times in answer to curious questions. Mum is always happy to answer questions; she says letting people ask is good because that way they get to learn things about Guide Dogs and people like her with vision impairment.

From that first day, we both understood each other. Our training together was supposed to take 7 days. We were allocated a room together at the live-in training centre of Guide Dogs Queensland, where they run the lessons for the new Guide Dog handlers. Thanks to another COVID lockdown that was about to happen, we only spent 5 days at the training centre before I was sent home with Mum to a place called Toowoomba.

Guide Dog Queensland requires that new handlers and dogs spend the first two weeks building their unique bond of trust and understanding. The entire Queensland community was in lockdown which meant Mum and I were forced to stay home getting to know each other. I had never been allowed on a chair, bed, or sofa before, so I loved that Mum immediately let me on the furniture. Furniture is much more comfortable than being on the floor.

We are inseparable partners, working together to navigate the world around us. Mum relies on me for guidance and support, and in return, I provide unwavering loyalty and companionship. Our bond is special. Unique, unlike any other, built on trust and mutual respect for each other.

I can go almost anywhere with Mum; my papers say I can. I have a feeling that reading must be a hard task for humans because Mum often gets refused access because of me. Overhearing Mum's conversations, I might be wrong about the reading bit. Perhaps it's got nothing to do with reading. Perhaps not everyone wants to understand the law, or maybe they think it's okay to ignore it.

"It is hard to believe that despite Guide Dogs having been in Australia for over 50 years and the legislation that is in place, we are still experiencing discrimination on a regular basis," Mum wrote in her first book, Running for My Life. "There is a 99% chance I will be refused entry because of Keegan. In rare instances, it is genuinely a lack of awareness."

My Mum is savvy. People make the mistake of thinking that she's not entirely all there because she has low vision.

That she's not that smart. But let me tell you, my Mum is definitely smart. She's kind and generous but does not allow herself to be a pushover or be taken advantage of.

I'm proud that Mum knows how to handle herself in the media, whether in front of the cameras or on the radio. Did you know she used to be a model and an actress? She was a tattoo model in Sydney and has many amazing stories to share about who she worked with and the fun stuff she used to do. Of course, that was before I came into her life.

Because there is nothing wrong with Mum's eyes, she does not actually look blind. I don't know the whole story, but it's all in the first book about how she became low vision. Special aids include glasses that can talk, recognise features, and speak to Mum, allowing her to move about confidently. At home, we are great mates; I don't have to wear my harness, so I can run around the house and yard. I get to play, sleep on Mum's bed, and sit on the couch beside her when she's feeling upset.

I love all the adventures that Mum and I have together. The parkrun is so much fun, and everyone welcomes us there. It's a happy place for us both. I think that's because no one judges, and we are both just accepted for who we are.

Since Mum and I got paired up, you will not believe what I have seen. People can be so insensitive and downright mean. Mum might seem tough, but underneath it all, she's a gentle soul. Her confidence gets battered when people say mean things about her or me. But she's a fighter. She's a fighter because that's one thing she has learnt to do. To stand up for her own rights. Once, long ago, she used to be meek and mild, afraid to say anything or draw attention to herself.

She's still that shy person on the inside; I see it when we are home together, and she's sitting quietly alone.

People think Mum is tough, but she's not. She's a softie who gets sad and upset when we are turned away from places. It's not nice when we can't have breakfast or lunch at a café because ignorant people think I am a dog! I might look like an ordinary dog, but I have a special harness with the words Guide Dog across it; Mum always carries the official card to prove I am legit. No harness bought on Temu or eBay for me – I have the real deal from Guide Dogs Queensland.

I get offended when I see kids having tantrums and tossing food on the floor. I am not even allowed to eat anything when I am in my harness. Gosh, it is so tempting to lick the floors, but I have standards to maintain and a job that I need to do – keep Mum safe always.

Did you know, she's even had a bar built at home? A proper flash one. Mum says it's easier being at home than risking going out and being refused entry. Mind you, it doesn't smell half as bad as some of the bars I've been into. The bar at home is actually kind of nice. Not only does it smell good, but I also get to flop on the couch. If we were in a public bar, I'd have to wear my harness and be at work ready to listen for commands from Mum.

The rule for me when we are out is "all paws on the floor." People are not allowed to pat or talk to me while I am working. Working means looking after Mum. My job is to protect and keep her safe when she's out in the community. If someone talks to me, I might get distracted, and that's not safe as it would endanger Mum's life.

Finding Mum a seat and sitting quietly on the floor beside

her or under her chair, ready to spring to work whenever she gives me a command, is my focus. No sneaky snacks because I am not allowed to eat when in my uniform of the Guide Dog harness. I lay down in my harness minding my own business whilst Mum is having dinner at the restaurant or in a coffee shop. Quite often, people rudely start talking to me and wanting to pat me. Like, seriously do I go and wake your baby up to see if it's having a good sleep!!!

"Never bend your head. Always hold it high. Look the world straight in the eye."

Helen Keller

Perceptions

As an individual who loves to get out and about, I felt that having a Guide Dog would make my life so much easier; my love of travel comes from having been controlled for much of my life.

My perception was that Keegan would make my life easier. Places that had previously been almost impossible for me to navigate would become accessible. It was only after my lived first-hand experience that I am now able to express the view that even though Keegan does a great job and is a wonderful companion, the reality is that he makes it harder for me to enter public places without having to think about whether I am going to have a fight on my hands. It is a lot harder for one reason only: the discrimination and ignorance we experience daily.

Disability is part of human diversity. It is disheartening to experience, on an almost daily basis, prejudice, and mistreatment due to ignorance and societal misconceptions.

Despite legislation and campaigns that promote inclusivity and accessibility, there exists, as I have discovered through my personal experiences, a massive stigma, prejudice, and discrimination towards someone with a Guide Dog.

Before Keegan came into my life, I would attend appointments in person. There was no trouble with transport. I could get into a car or a taxi without worry of refusal. Today, if it is at all possible, I choose to conduct all my appointments online. I have also taken to doing more online grocery shopping.

There is an upside to online grocery shopping as you see the totals added up as you shop rather than having to do manually add up to make sure I am not over budget.

Don't get me wrong, with Keegan by my side to guide me; it is definitely safer, easier and extremely pleasant to go for a walk to welcoming local places. Keegan guides me to cross the roads, prompts me to stop at curbs, lets me know when there are oncoming cars, helps me up and down the stairs, guides me to find a seat, and so much more. Keegan is my mate; he makes me get out of bed each day, and he motivates me because he needs to go to the toilet and exercise. I love having him in my life.

On the mental level, life with Keegan has become more stressful because society does not abide by the laws that exist to protect us from discrimination. There seems to be a presumption that because I am blind, I will not pursue a case of discrimination.

This assumption is not only totally false but also harmful. It is my personal belief that it is crucial to accept that people with disabilities have the same rights as everyone else. In navigating the challenges that I am not alone in facing, it is important that I take the time to educate others on the laws in place to protect against discrimination based on disability. By raising awareness and advocating for equality, I believe that I am working towards a more inclusive and understanding society where individuals from all races, backgrounds and abilities are treated with respect and dignity. We have the right to speak up and demand fair treatment, regardless of our differences or challenges.

As someone with limited vision who relies on a Guide Dog, I am acutely aware of how perceptions and discrimination are deeply connected. In fact, I would say they are intertwined in certain situations.

I have often pondered how others with Guide Dogs cope. I've now discovered that many Guide Dog handlers live to a set routine, staying within the confines of where they feel safe and going to the same places each week. By safe, I mean welcoming of Guide Dogs. There is no fear of being refused.

When writing this book, I considered whether to mention businesses that discriminated against Keegan and me by denying us entry. After much contemplation, although I discuss refusals, I do not name the establishments for the most part. I chose to focus on the positive experiences and shout out the wonderful places that welcomed us warmly and provided outstanding service.

When I was younger, I did not have a voice. I was afraid to speak out for fear of repercussions, but that has now changed. Having found my voice means that I feel a deep responsibility to use my voice to call out injustices and strive to create a world where everyone is treated with dignity and respect. We need to foster a community where discrimination has no place to thrive. It's a continuous process of standing up for what is right and advocating for those who cannot speak out. The behaviour of those who denied us entry or service has generally stemmed from either ignorance of the law or, more concerning, a belief that they are exempt coupled with a complete refusal to accept the evidence.

It is unfortunate that some individuals choose to deny entry or service based on ignorance or a misguided sense of superiority. Changing these perceptions is only possible through education and awareness. By continuing to advocate for my rights and providing evidence of the law, I am actively working towards a more inclusive and understanding society rather than sitting at home and accepting the status quo.

I always travel with a supply of information cards provided by the Queensland government that clearly outline how to identify Guide, Hearing & Assistance Dogs.

The card clearly states, "Certified guide, hearing and assistance dogs are specially trained to do important tasks for their handler and have similar rights to people when accessing public places, public transport, and places of accommodation. This includes the right to access shops, cinemas, hospitality venues, rental and holiday accommodation, taxis, aircraft, public transport and entertainment and sporting facilities."

Additionally, "The Guide, Hearing and Assistance Dogs Act 2009 confirms these rights and fines apply to individuals or businesses that deny such access; refuse to serve the handler; separate the hander from their dog; or charge extra for the dog." It also contains information on identifying a certified dog, including "Handlers accompanied by a certified dog will carry an identity card."

My first action when refused entry is to ask to speak to the manager in an attempt to clarify the situation. I offer the information card, but sadly, most are not interested. It's a fairly normal reaction to be told to "Fuck Off" or "Get Out."

Changing perceptions needs to be a priority. To refuse to accept this evidence and refuse us entry is why I have no hesitation in lodging a discrimination complaint. I find the process taxing and daunting, but I am determined to continue pushing for better awareness and education.

The fines can be up to 100 penalty units and the current rate of a penalty unit in Queensland, at the time of writing this book, is $143. That's a fine of $14,300. I do not want to see anyone fined and would prefer education.

The laws already exist to protect us from discrimination. Enforcing the laws is another matter. After all, unless a complaint is made and action is taken, there is no repercussion on the business or individual refusing us entry. Nothing will change.

Without effective enforcement of existing laws, discrimination will and does continue to persist. It is important for anyone who believes in equality to be vigilant and speak up against any form of discrimination they witness. It is not an easy thing to do.

It might be simple, but simple and easy are two different things. It is my hope that by raising awareness, holding those who discriminate accountable, and doing my bit towards working to create a more educated society, there is hope for a time in the not-too-distant future where everyone is treated with dignity and respect.

Unfortunately, not everyone with a Guide Dog has the energy or drive to pursue legal avenues. I take encouragement from the positive messages from others who have faced the same discrimination. It is heartening to know that these are sources of support and inspiration for those facing discrimination.

While legal action may not be the right path for everyone, the power of solidarity and community can make a significant impact. By sharing experiences and offering encouragement, we can create a more inclusive and understanding world for all individuals, including those with Guide Dogs. Every voice and every story contributes to creating a positive change and maintaining awareness.

I am always encouraged when I receive messages from people I do not know that confirm I am making a difference by standing up for my rights. *"I have an assistance dog and face discrimination and ignorance constantly. Hubby and I are so grateful for you being so brave and making a stand".* It seems not everyone has the energy to make their voices heard, and I totally get that.

In a world where silence can often feel like the easier path, I have chosen to use the power of my voice. Mine is a voice of resilience forged through years of being stifled. It is not just about fighting for my own rights but about paving the way for a future where injustices are challenged, and change is embraced.

With each battle I fight, I know deep down that the ripple effect extends beyond myself, hopefully impacting those still finding their courage. This journey is not just mine and Keegan's; it needs to be a collective of voices joining together, united in the pursuit of challenging discriminatory behaviour.

I put up a fight when I encounter inappropriate behaviour. After many years of being suppressed and afraid to make my voice heard, I make sure that I use it now that I have finally discovered my voice. Not just to change things for me, but it is more a case of working towards a great awareness so conditions improve for others who may not have the energy or confidence to stand up to injustices.

My eyes look perfect. They are clear, bright, and, I am told, attractive. The only problem is they do not work. How I lost my sight is a long story covered in my first book; the abridged version is that it is the result of brain surgery. Because I had previously been sighted and have worked as a model and actress, with my sight deteriorating over several years, I am able to walk confidently (albeit sometimes into things). I am trained to look directly at a speaker, giving the impression that I am sighted.

"You lying piece of dog shit, there's a bullet somewhere with your name on it and a nice warm place in hell for people like you. You are offensive to people with a real disability," appeared on social media as a result of one case of intense publicity that followed a refusal.

Am I frightened by this kind of threat? Yes. Most definitely.

I live on my own with Keegan. As a trained Guide Dog, he does not display aggressive behaviour such as growling, biting, or even raising hackles. If he had displayed any of these, he would not have passed the Public Access Test

(PAT), which is necessary for him to work as a Guide Dog. Thankfully, I have a fully secure house with security cameras fitted both inside and around the outside perimeter for my protection. The inside cameras have been invaluable as evidence when I have been threatened by a support worker.

Discrimination exists on many levels, and often, we do not realise that it is a pervasive issue that affects many aspects of our lives, from social interactions to employment opportunities. We often do not think that our actions or words are discriminatory, making it even more insidious and difficult to address.

I can now see that I was discriminated against as a child by the school I attended and through the years of my marriage when I was trying to flee a domestic violence situation and a volatile husband. Not for a second did I register that I was being discriminated against. I did not know any different; it was only when the TAFE refused to let me continue with one of my classes that I began to think about discrimination.

Reflecting on those experiences, I understand the importance of being aware of different forms of discrimination. It is a complex issue that can begin to manifest in subtle ways, often going unnoticed until it directly affects us. Each person's journey is unique, and the lessons we learn shape our perceptions and understanding of the world.

Some forms of discrimination that are often overlooked yet have a significant impact. Ageism is a common discrimination that you may have experienced yourself; being too young or too old. It can happen in the workplace, where older workers are passed over for promotions or job opportunities, or in social settings, where younger people may be dismissed as immature or inexperienced.

Ableism is obviously my pet peeve, as this is discrimination against people with disabilities. It can take many forms, such as physical barriers that prevent people from accessing certain places or services, or attitudes and beliefs that treat people with disabilities as inferior or less capable.

Colourism is discrimination based on skin colour. It often seems to be that in Australia, people with lighter skin are favoured over those with darker skin, which is simply ridiculous given the multicultural society that this country is.

Discrimination against Guide Dogs is a new area many do not think of. Indeed, I never thought about it until I had my own Guide Dog. It is important that we recognise the value of Guide Dogs and ensure that they are treated with the respect and dignity they deserve.

Rocking a canvas of tattoos, I'm no stranger to perceptions, judgements and stereotypes that come with flaunting body ink. Beneath the vibrant colours and designs on my body lies a story. Each tattoo etched into my skin represents a chapter of my life, a memory, a symbol of my journey. They are not just inked on flesh; they reflect who I am, my passions, my dreams, and my struggles.

My tattoos are a road map of my experiences, a visual diary, a souvenir, and a gallery of my personal growth. Each stroke of the needle was a decision made with intention, a choice to inscribe a piece of my identity onto my canvas permanently.

They are not just decorations; they are a form of self-expression, a way to communicate without words. The tattoos are a testament to my decision to embrace my true self, to stand out rather than blend in, to declare to the world boldly: this is me, unapologetically. When you look at my tattoos, see beyond the ink and lines; see the stories, the passions, the essence of who I am. I am a woman with a voice that I am determined to use to shine a light on injustices.

Have you ever stopped to think about how we perceive life or situations around us? It's interesting to consider that all our thoughts, beliefs, and opinions are perceptions. Interestingly, the older I become, the more of the world I visit, the more people I meet and situations I experience the more my perceptions change. That is no doubt because perceptions are shaped by each experience we encounter and go through.

All manner of experiences influence our perceptions; even more interesting is that we have external perceptions that are often visually triggered. These include things like the colour of our skin, ethnicity, and external features, including our manner of dress, hairstyles, and tattoos.

I have heard it said that it is my tattooed body that is the cause of the discrimination that I experience. That's simply not true. Other Guide Dog handlers are going through similar experiences of being refused entry into public places.

"I may be blind, but I have a vision of where I want to be. I may be weak, but I have the strength to achieve anything."

Janice Whittle

Freedom to Travel

For much of my early life, I did not have the freedom to travel. Shackled to a marriage where I did not dare express an opinion, let alone deviate from the route my husband permitted, I could not travel freely. Expressing my opinion was forbidden. The repercussions were severe and I was trapped in fear.

Once I dug deep and found the courage to break free from my marriage and all the constraints that bound me, I discovered the joy of travel as I ran for my life. A vast, uncharted territory opened up in front of me, waiting to be explored. Each new destination filled me with a sense of liberation. No longer tied to my past, I embraced the opportunities to travel.

Exploring new places and travelling whenever the opportunity presents itself has become a way to reclaim my voice and, most importantly, my independence. Travel is now a huge and integral part of my life. I have nothing keeping me at home. No family to draw me back home or keep me tied to a specific place. I fought for my freedom as I ran in fear for my life.

Having been deliberately kept short of money for much of my early life has resulted in me becoming extremely savvy when it comes to managing my finances. Living a comfortable but thrifty daily life, including being happy to shop where bargains are on offer for groceries and clothing, combined with being minimalist when it comes to possessions, allows me to save up for travel adventures.

One of my top tactics is pairing up with others to bulk buy and save money. Using a support worker to drive Keegan and myself because it is just too difficult to try and get a cab, I make a point of doing a circuit each month to places I know offer fantastic budget-extending deals. Shopping this way extends my pension dollars and ensures I have the ingredients to prepare nutritious meals that keep my body well-sustained. These deals are open to everyone and not just those on a pension.

Today, I am free to go wherever the spirit moves me to explore. Travel is not just a passion for me; it is a way of life, a constant reminder of the beauty and diversity that exist in our world. I have been fortunate to visit bustling cities, quiet villages, and breathtaking landscapes while running for my life after leaving Australia to find safety. Each place I visited has left indelible memories imprinted on my soul. The people I met along the way taught me invaluable lessons and broadened my perspective. Every journey I continue to take provides new experiences.

Sadly, since Keegan has come into my life, I have started to experience discrimination as I travel. The soul-stirring adventures that transform my life, and which I desperately look forward to, have become more challenging with a Guide Dog.

####

On my first road trip to Emerald, I stayed at the Irish Village, which has since had a name change. They were fantastic, but discrimination was everywhere. I had not expected that.

Feeling like a Chinese meal, we headed to the nearest restaurant; it was two doors down from where we were staying. We were immediately refused entry as soon as they saw Keegan despite the fact a patron in the restaurant backed me up. I grabbed a takeaway menu on the way out so I had details of where we had been.

At the second Chinese place, the young waitress took us to a table and seated us. Not long after, she returned to our table accompanied by what I guessed were the owners, who stood over me and insisted that we must leave. Keegan was quietly under my chair while the demands to leave became more insistent. Knowing we were not going to be served a meal, we left. No dinner for us that night.

The following day, we walked into the local pub and again were refused entry. Feeling totally deflated after being refused entry into three venues within a 24-hour period, I did not know what to do. I decided to complain to the local Council. It was the first time I had ever done that. I went straight up to the desk. I knew what I wanted.

"I want to speak to your solicitor right now," I was straightforward. "And I am not leaving until I do."

"What's the problem?" asked the receptionist.

"Every place I've been in so far has refused my guide dog and that's against the law." I was pretty steamed up. "I want legal right now."

"We don't have anyone here," she said.

"Then I want to speak to your disability access officer. I am not leaving till this is sorted out."

The receptionist scurried off and returned with a woman who introduced herself as the librarian and asked if I wanted to talk in reception or preferred a private room. I chose the private room as I did not want everyone hearing what I had to say, I was blunt and angry. I explained what had been happening.

"They can't do that!" was her shocked response. I gave her the names of the three businesses, and she instructed me to return to my hotel room and wait to hear from her.

As good as her word, she telephoned me a couple of hours later with a list of places that she could guarantee would allow Keegan and me access. It was wrong that I was made to feel unwelcome, and although her actions were supposed to help, it was wrong that she had to go to those extremes of telephoning around the town.

The list she provided was varied and ranged across price points. I tried the café and the 5-star restaurant, which is not something I would normally splurge on, but I wanted to check it out for myself. The librarian had not presumed what my budget was and had given me respect by offering me choices.

On my way to Longreach, I received a phone call from the librarian letting me know that she had also been in touch with the Food Handling & Safety authorities and that they would be paying a visit to the establishments that had refused us service. At the on the spot inspection they would also be reminding them of the rights of a Guide Dog.

A few months later, I was back in Emerald for another parkrun, and I made a point to visit the Chinese restaurant; Blind Citizens Australia encourages us to revisit places we have lodged complaints about to see whether there have been changes made.

"Guide Dog!" shouted the young boy behind the counter as soon as we stepped in the door.

"Identification!" snapped the woman who had come rushing out from the back. Reaching into my backpack, I pulled out my handler's card and handed it to her for inspection.

"You want same table?" she handed back the card and begrudgingly escorted us to the same table we'd been evicted from a few months earlier. Yes, things had changed.

In April 2022, I completed the Mt Isa parkrun and went in search of breakfast. There was not a great deal to choose from and it was also Easter weekend which meant everywhere was either closed or packed. I went to a café not far from where we had done our run. Keegan found a table in the corner which was great because we don't like sitting out in the centre. It is better to be out of the way. Keegan went under the table as I sat in my chair, and my support worker was opposite me.

As we were looking at the menu a female staff member came over and asked if we would like to start with any drinks.

"Can I have a hot chocolate please skim milk?" my support worker ordered a latte; then she must have looked down.

"You have a dog?"

"Yes, I do."

"You have to go and sit outside."

" Well, no, he's a Guide Dog. He's legally allowed to be

here. You can see he is in his harness. You can see that. I have identification that states that we are legally allowed in here."

She was insistent that we go outside. I asked for her name.

"My name is Nadia," came the abrupt reply.

"Well, Nadia, I would like to speak to the manager."

Her total tone changed. "I am the manager."

"Well," I responded, "the shit just hit the fan, didn't it!" She walked off. I thought that was the end of the matter and continued to look at the menu.

"I have just spoken to the assistant manager, and we both agree that your dog has to be outside."

I began to state the Disability Discrimination Act and the fact they could be fined for turning us away. She continued to insist I leave.

Trying to control myself, I thought, "I'm not going to make a scene." As I got up to leave. Two steps later, I could not restrain myself any longer.

The place was packed, it was a national chain café with 360 outlets, I was furious. I spoke at the top of my voice. "Excuse me, everybody. A blind lady is being kicked out because she has a Guide Dog. Do not support this business." I was actually pretty restrained considering all I wanted to say.

Sitting in our car which was just across the road, a guy ran up to me and grabbed the door so I could not close it. "Please, come inside. Everyone wants you inside." I responded that the management didn't want me there. "We're leaving and I'm going to lodge a complaint."

"My mate owns the cafe. I'll call him now."

I thought I'll do the right thing and see what happened. He rang his mate, but there was no answer; considering it was

Easter Saturday and a long weekend, that was not entirely surprising.

"Please, can I have your number?" he asked after he had tried and tried and tried the number but couldn't get an answer.

I would normally never give my name and number but because I knew that if it went to court, it would show that I did try and resolve the issue. I gave this guy my name and number. Once again he asked me to please come back anyway. I declined.

On Easter Sunday I got a phone call from the owner. He was appalled at how I had been treated.

"Please, I'm happy to shout you breakfast tomorrow." It would be Easter Monday. I accepted the offer but insisted he text me with the value of the breakfast because I wanted to protect myself and have it in writing. At the end of our conversation, he said, "We'd really like you to come back, and we apologise, but more importantly, while you are there, could you please apologise to Nadia because you really upset her."

I'm like, what the fuck? Why should I apologise to her? She unlawfully told me to leave. I told him in no uncertain terms that I definitely would not be apologising. In fact, she needed to apologise to me.

"If I go tomorrow, will there be any trouble?" I was concerned and needed assurance. He assured me there would not be and as good as his word, sent a voucher for $60 to cover breakfast the next morning.

"Right," I primed my friend, "we're going to spend $59.99. No more. We are not going over $60. They deserve none of my money."

The next morning, Keegan who is always ahead of me obviously, started walking into the café. A male staff member came up and said, "Sorry, dogs aren't allowed. You have to go outside."

"Really?" I turned to walk out, thinking I'd just go straight to court.

"Oh, no, no, come inside." It was Nadia, the manager from Saturday. "Come inside. Come inside. Please come inside."

We sat at the same table in the corner where we had been on Saturday morning. When it came time to pay the bill, we discovered the 15% public holiday surcharge. The surcharge took the bill to over the $59.99 that we had calculated. I kicked myself for trying to be smart as I got my credit card out, prepared to pay up. Nadia waived the extra charges, saying it was all covered while also offering me an apology for the treatment on our previous visit.

Small towns are notorious for refusals. It makes life difficult when there are limited places to get a meal. A pizza takeaway in Mt Isa also refused us entry. I mean, a pizza joint with no seating and a counter to order from!

####

During my June 2022 visit to Airlie Beach and Proserpine, I found the security at the doors of all the pubs and hotels turned us away. They even phoned ahead to let one another know Keegan and I were heading down the street towards them - I know this because I overheard the conversations.

Thankfully, we had no problem with our accommodation,

which was the YHA local hostel, where we were welcomed like all other guests.

There was a strange bar across from the hotel. It had kinky kinds of "cells" with female patrons dancing on the bar and tables getting their gear off. This place welcomed us as they had a different company running security. Once again, it was in a minority group that we found acceptance.

I did inform Blind Citizens Australia of the problem, and I understand that they spoke with the security firm. I never bothered to go back to test whether Keegan and I would be allowed entry as I am quite timid, and it takes a lot from me, mentally and emotionally, to challenge our refusals.

I had not expected the level of discrimination we faced because Guide Dogs have been around for umpteen years. The first Guide Dog arrived in Australia in 1950 from the UK with a man called Dr Arnold Cook. By 1957, there were Guide Dog Associations across the country. That's over 65 years, and I naively expected everyone would know the law by now.

We all know it is against the law to speed, to stab someone, to steal from a shop, and to refuse a Guide Dog. We all know we must wear a seatbelt or face a fine. Considering that adults own and operate the public venues where the discrimination occurs, I feel that it is not unrealistic to expect them to be educated enough to be aware of the law. I was wrong. It never ceases to amaze me how little knowledge and awareness exists among the general public.

Thrilled at being paired with Keegan, I was excited and started to look forward to being part of a wider world with great accessibility, thanks to the extra support that a Guide

Dog would provide. I thought life was going to be hunky dory. I rang Guide Dogs Queensland when I experienced my first refusal, hoping they could offer some support and advice. I'm paraphrasing, but the bottom line was that although this happened, it was not their problem; their only job was to train the dogs to offer handlers an independent life. They are not involved with any issues that occur on the discrimination front once the dog has been matched and handed over. As the refusals continued, I came to the realisation that I was on my own with Keegan. If I wanted to go out and about, I was the only one responsible for sorting out our problems.

To say I was shocked is an understatement. There is a huge gap around awareness and education relating to the rights of a Guide Dog and their handlers.

In a harness, Keegan knows he is in work mode and is trained to give me the freedom and confidence to step into a world that was previously not so easily accessible. We have been perfectly matched, and he is highly skilled in assisting me with everyday living. He helps me navigate busy streets, avoid obstacles, and keeps me safe. Following a strict routine in his work environment is essential to my safety.

Both of us love to walk as it helps us both stay healthy and fit, but there are also many times when we need public transport. Sadly, it is not easy getting a car to take us from point A to point B.

It has got to the stage where I dread going out anywhere that will involve me needing to rely on a taxi to get home again. It is the everyday little items that add up to being a mammoth hurdle. For instance, Keegan and I can walk to the shops, but we need a taxi to return home with our groceries.

To get to and from the airport, to catch flights, to reach a medical appointment and so the list goes on. Calling a taxi is something much of the population takes for granted.

13Cabs is a taxi company that I have been forced to take to the Human Rights Commission due to taxi drivers' consistent refusal to accept me into their cars because I have a Guide Dog.

I had a flight booked from Adelaide to Brisbane on May 22nd, 2023. After the flight landed, we collected our luggage and proceeded to the taxi rank. The taxi marshal told us to go to stand number 7. We were there less than 2 minutes when the taxi approached. The taxi driver flipped the boot open, and the driver and my support worker put the luggage in the boot. The driver then said there was no room in the boot for my Guide Dog, so Keegan would have to be left behind.

Aghast, we informed the taxi driver that Keegan was a registered Guide Dog and would sit in the foot well, NOT the boot. The driver stated he did not have to accept my Guide Dog. He said when he filled out the form to become a taxi driver, he ticked the box to 'no dogs' and therefore, in his mind, he did not have to accept Keegan. The argument became aggressive, so much so that the taxi marshal stepped in to tell the driver that Keegan must be accepted in the taxi. The driver argued with the taxi marshal. The taxi driver parked at taxi stand 8, approached the arguing pair, and told the taxi driver refusing Keegan that as it was a Guide Dog, he had no choice and must accept the dog.

The driver refused; the taxi marshal ordered the driver to leave the airport with no fare and told him not to return. A security guard came out due to the arguments and asked me what happened. I explained that the driver was refusing service to me and my guide dog.

"This happens quite often here." The security officer shared.

The arguing driver drove off, and thankfully, a decent driver was there immediately who flipped the boot open and put all of the luggage in the boot. Keegan sat at my feet in the foot well, I was shaken and distraught.

I lodged a complaint with 13Cabs which has not been treated seriously. It's also annoying that 13Cabs don't seem to want to assist in this complaint but yet they have information on their website stating that it is against the law to refuse a service dog. I have a video of the driver refusing service and arguing. I also have photos of the taxi and the individual driver.

I consider going to Human Rights and pursuing my complaint through the legal system as a last resort step. In the case of the taxi company, their response to my complaint was that their entire fleet of drivers was required to complete Induction Training and that the section on Transporting Our Passengers with Confidence and Care covered transporting disabled and able-bodied passengers.

They added that if a driver breaches the Code of Conduct regarding transporting customers, they are required to complete Values Training at a cost of $220 to the driver; if there was a case of a repeat offence, the driver's accreditation might be cancelled.

On 9 December 2023 Blind Citizens Australia - Queensland branch, sent out an email to all its members with advice on how to consider dealing with the issue of taxi transport.

Subject: *Ensuring a Smooth Taxi Experience for Dog Guide Users*

Dear BCA Queensland Members,

We hope this message finds you well. Today, we'd like to address a recurring concern some of our members have faced when using taxis, specifically regarding individuals with dog Guides being refused service by taxi drivers.

After a Constructive conversation with a taxi driver occurred earlier in the year, a potential solution emerged...

Informing the taxi operator about your vision impairment and the presence of a dog guide when booking a ride. This information is then included in the job notes, ensuring that drivers who accept the job are already aware of the dog guide.

We understand that many of you may feel hesitant about disclosing your disability, and we respect your right to privacy. Additionally, we understand the law around your right to take a dog guide with you in a taxi. However, we believe that the benefits of informing the operator about your dog guide may far outweigh any potential discomfort.

By sharing this information, you contribute to a smoother and more inclusive transportation experience. The driver will be prepared for your dog guide, and this proactive step can help prevent any issues upon their arrival.

Your well-being and convenience are our top priority, and we strive to create a community that supports each other. If you have any concerns or suggestions regarding this matter, please feel free to reach out.

Thank you for being part of BCA Queensland and for your continued support in fostering an inclusive and supportive community."

They added the caveat *"The above is sent only as considered "advice" so please receive it as such."*

My personal experience, which several other Guide Dog owners also share, is that the result is that drivers refuse to accept the job, and we are still without transport.

I am part of a social media group for Guide Dog handlers, and way too many people with guide, hearing or assistance dogs are refused service every day by Uber and taxi drivers. Posts such as those below are all too common.

"My worst taxi refuse refusal day, thus far, was yesterday, waiting at Flinders Street Station taxi rank in Melbourne. I had three refusals in a row, and the fourth taxi wouldn't leave until they got confirmation from the head office that they could take a Guide Dog."

"I had a taxi driver who left me, my daughter and my son in the rain once he saw my dog. He said he was going to park the car and drove off. I tried to call 13 cabs. And I was told to call the next day. I rang the police assistance line. I was told to wait at home and the police would come to my house to take a statement. I got a call from the local police saying that wasn't a refusal."

"I've got three refusals since the beginning of the year, and that was in February last year. So in two months, I had three refusals.

And two of them were assist drivers where they get paid extra to assist you get in and out of the car."

These situations occur all too often across Australia. They should not happen today, with legislation in place to protect us.

ABC News carried a story on Henry Macphillamy on 15 February 2023, and I share a small excerpt below to emphasize that this is not uncommon.

"A Brisbane man who has been refused service via a rideshare company three times in the past two months says he is "tired" of having to stand up for his "basic rights as a human being".

He said in most cases, the rideshare driver would cancel the job once they found out an animal would be travelling too, but the driver in question had not seen that information until too late.

"I advised him he was breaking the law and that I'd report him and I did," Mr Macphillamy said.

"My frustration is that this stuff keeps happening."

"It's my view that it's not being very heavily regulated and in the situation where rideshare is making itself an indispensable part of the economy, there doesn't seem to be a social licence for them and drivers are doing whatever they want."

Uber offered an apology and a $35 credit for future rides but Mr Macphillamy was left feeling that the refusal was the "final straw".

Keegan and I have shared similar experiences. Our most recent experience was on 16 March 2024, after I attended a St Patrick's Eve Dinner. I regularly attend this annual formal event each year, which I look forward to for weeks ahead. Keegan and I both get frocked up in our best green outfits, which, given that I do not have that many chances in the year to get dressed up makes the occasion extra special.

I feel a deep connection to my roots and the rich traditions of Ireland. It's a time to celebrate the vibrant culture, music, and history of the Emerald Isle where I was born. I enjoy a pint of Guinness and rejoice in celebrating in the Irish spirit on St Patrick's Eve, which also happens to be the eve of my birthday.

After having a wonderful night, I ordered an Uber to get home. A car pulled up, and the number plates matched my booking, so I got in the car with Keegan. The driver immediately told me I was in the wrong car and insisted that I get out.

"Nope, I'm in the right Uber." I showed him my booking equally determined that I was not about to get out of the car.

"You didn't order an Uber Pet, so you have to get out", was his retort.

I was trying to find a way to resolve the situation and knew that standing my ground was important. I didn't want to cause more trouble than necessary. Looking out at the empty street, I pondered my options. I had none. The rest of the dinner guests had gone as their own transport had arrived whilst I was arguing inside the car with the driver. If I got out, I knew I would be stranded in the dark, most likely, for hours on end. The argument went on. I refused to get out of the car. I knew my rights and I also knew that the likelihood of getting another car to take me home was slim.

As the tension in the car escalated, I took a deep breath

before pulling out my phone to start recording the disagreement stating that Keegan was a Guide Dog, not a pet, and therefore had a legal right to be in the car.

Eventually the driver gave up and began to drive us on our journey home.

'Yep, I win, so I'll stop recording now', was the thought that passed through my head as I went to press the switch off recording button. Well, stupid me then realised that I had missed the button and had not actually recorded anything!

When we finally pulled up outside my house, I felt a deep sense of relief wash over me. I did not realise how on edge I had been for the entire 30-minute ride home. After making sure the doors were firmly locked and my alarms on, Keegan and I went to bed where I fell into an exhausted sleep.

The next morning, I received the Uber invoice. The driver had the cheek to charge me a waiting fee to compensate for his time wasted arguing over my right to have my Guide Dog in the car.

Uber has been an ongoing issue and I was pleased to recently be included in a consultation that has resulted in Uber now cracking down on drivers refusing passengers with assistance animals. Teaming up with Vision Australia they have create a course for all drivers to reinforce the laws that are in place to protect those of us with assistance animals.

I was heartened to hear that on the Uber website, Emma Foley, Director of Mobility Operations at Uber Australia and New Zealand said: *"Assistance animal refusal is unacceptable, yet it's a consistent issue in the industry. By implementing new measures focused on ensuring all drivers are aware of their obligations, and consequences for those that ignore them, we hope to prevent this happening as much as possible,"*

"This new education is not set and forget. Through continued monitoring and engagement with our driver-partners and the disability community, we will assess our progress and work to keep reducing instances of service animal refusals on the Uber platform."

"In the past few years, we know that some riders with assistance animals have felt disheartened with their experience on the Uber platform, after being refused trips by drivers because they're travelling with an assistance animal," Uber's director of mobility operations Emma Foley said.

"This is simply unacceptable. Riders with assistance animals have the same rights as any rider to access the services they need, including being able to book any kind of Uber trip, and travel with their assistance animal from A to B.

"By implementing new measures focused on ensuring all drivers are aware of their obligations, and consequences for those that ignore them, we hope to prevent this happening as much as possible."

How do I solve the problem of getting around? I can't. It is a challenge that raises its head frequently, given that I am consistently on the move, visiting different places. Where possible, I try to engage the services of a support worker under my NDIS plan who will act as a driver for Keegan and myself, but this is not always a practical solution depending on the days and the locations.

On my visit to Proserpine, I needed to use a shuttle service as no other transport was available.

"How many seats would you like?"

"Well, two. One is for me, and one is for my guide dog."

It was then that the woman on the other end of the phone said, "We don't allow dogs." Despite my stating that Keegan was a Guide Dog and legally allowed on the transport, her response came back, "We do not allow any animals. This is a luxury service. We do not allow any animals at all. We do not want your Guide Dog on our bus."

Feeling aggrieved, I rang Blind Citizens Australia. "Tell me what happened, Janice." I have become well acquainted with the staff as I regularly call to lodge complaints. I told him, and shortly after, I got a call back from the shuttle service.

"We do not allow dogs on our luxury shuttle service. But in your case, okay."

I never went ahead with the luxury shuttle because I felt totally uncomfortable. They would only take me because Blind Citizens Australia had clearly come down hard on them. I was not welcome and certainly did not want to be sitting on a bus feeling totally alienated. It is extremely saddening that it had to come down to having a legal entity, like Blind Citizens Australia, forcing acceptance where it was clearly not welcome. Ultimately, I found a personal driver who was prepared to drive myself and Keegan while we were in Proserpine for the parkrun.

Interestingly, I have discovered that the police can issue a fine to anyone refusing us transport or admission to a public place. The key word is public. However, the police do not seem to be totally clear on this matter themselves, as when I have been to make complaints, the reactions I have received have ranged from, "Go away, this is a disability matter and we have real crimes to work on," to apologetic mumbles that they have to look into whether they have that power under the law.

I will be fair and say that the police at Morayfield did call me back after investigating the legalities of my complaint.

"Would you like to come back to the station and write a report?" The officer explained that he had investigated further and found that it is indeed against the law under both the Transport Act and the Disability Discrimination Act for anyone to refuse a Guide Dog.

When important information like that is not known to the authorities, it is alarming. I'd go so far as to say it is actually scary, truly concerning and makes me realise how much work needs to be done to educate and change public perceptions.

The situation with the police highlights the need for more awareness and education within society in general. By shedding light on these gaps in knowledge, we can work towards creating a more informed and inclusive community.

Education is crucial in shaping public perceptions and fostering a better understanding. It is my hope that this book will play a small part in shining the spotlight in what is a dark but rather large corner.

Cruising

In May 2021, I took my first trip to Longreach, in the far central west of Queensland. I went to do a parkrun and decided that while I was there it would be fun to go on a Thomson River sunset cruise.

The local information centre, a booking office for most tours in the area, called the cruise company to book for us only to be told that Keegan would not be allowed on board despite being a Guide Dog.

"That's very unusual" responded the woman I spoke to at the local Council office when I lodged my complaint. I also put up a post on my social media account about the refusal and tagged the company, too.

"Leave this with me, go back to your hotel and I'll be in touch," advised the Council officer.

When I left the Council officer, I checked my phone and saw that I had received a PM on Facebook from the cruise company asking for my contact details "I'd value an opportunity to speak directly and sort this out."

My phone rang as I lay on the bed back at the hotel, feeling extremely dejected. It was the owner of Outback Aussie Tours, the boat tour company. "What are you doing tonight?"

"Going to the pub to get pissed" was on the tip of my tongue.

"How about I shout you a boat cruise tonight and a bottle of wine?" he was genuinely apologetic and explained the staff member had made an error in refusing Keegan.

We had a lovely evening on the cruise, and I cannot praise them highly enough for handling the error.

Each time I take Keegan on a cruise ship, we have to go through serious paperwork, including a 14-page Biosecurity document and vet checks. It is a lengthy process, but it means everything is in order, we are preapproved, and the cruise liner knows we are coming.

I love cruising and generally go from the Port of Brisbane. Cruise ships are also a place where we have experienced quite a bit of abuse and ignorance from other passengers and crew alike. Things like saying it's unfair that I can bring Keegan onto the cruise ship, and they can't bring their pet dog, cat, parrot, etc.

I also get genuinely curious and kind passengers who query where Keegan's toilet is; that is a valid question. The answer is that the ships have designated areas where he can toilet. It's the first thing I ask once we have boarded the ship.

A recent incident occurred when I boarded a ship in Sydney rather than Brisbane, which is my usual habit. This was a cruise company I had previously used without any issues; they had confirmed via email on 15th August, 2023 to acknowledge receipt of the Biosecurity clearance which I had forwarded.

On 4th November, I completed a local parkrun before taking a taxi to White Bay Cruise Terminal. As I went to hand in my luggage a staff member started patting Keegan. I asked her to stop as he was a working Guide Dog. I moved to the other end away from her and again a staff member went to pat Keegan. I firmly told her NO! as I handed my luggage over to be checked.

I made my way to find Keegan a toileting area only to discover there was absolutely nowhere for him to go. He would have to hold on until we boarded the cruise ship. As soon as we boarded the cruise ship, we made our way to the service desk and joined the queue. When it was my time to be served, I asked where the toileting area was for my Guide Dog.

"I don't know" responded the staff member. "I'll ask my manager". He went into the office behind him and returned shortly after with the response "There is no toileting area for your dog".

"Fine," I responded, "I'll get him to shit on the carpet," and walked away. The ship's information desk staff were dismissive and unhelpful, so much so that I wanted to get off before we had even pulled out of Sydney.

I made my way to find my support worker who was at the Dragon Lady Restaurant confirming our dining arrangements. He was being served by a lady and as I recounted my experience at the service desk, the manager of the restaurant informed us that all staff had been informed that there would be two Guide Dogs on the cruise ship, Keegan being one of them. She immediately rang through to another staff to express her concerns on my behalf.

We made our way to our cabin and shortly after, a male member of staff came to our cabin. He was apparently a senior ranking staff member, and for the purpose of anonymity, I shall called him John. He had been contacted by the staff at the Dragon Lady Restaurant. John personally showed me where two dog toileting areas were located on Deck 7. After thanking John for his kindness in personally showing me where to take Keegan, I made my way back to the guest service desk to ask about VIP seating at the shows for my vision impairment. The female staff member on duty assured me that she would get the entertainment manager to call me to arrange this. I was promised he would be in touch within a couple of hours. Luckily, I was not holding my breath waiting for the call, as it never came.

On Sunday, we decided we'd treat ourselves to a lunch at Luke's Bar and Grill which was a meal that we needed to pay for as it was not included in the cruise price. As we were leaving, a male staff member started calling for Keegan as he was guiding me out of the restaurant. My support worker told the staff member that Keegan was working and must not be interrupted whilst on the job.

By this time, I was thoroughly frustrated, had had enough of the rubbish, unprofessional service staff and terrible treatment. Back in my cabin I used the cruise app to provide feedback on my experience. I mentioned that I was never contacted by the entertainment manager, the staff constantly wanting to pat and play with Keegan, no dog toileting area information on arrival and terrible service at the guest service desk.

Within two hours of providing the feedback, the entertainment manager got in touch to assure me he would reserve two front-row seats for me and my support worker. He apologised for the delayed response but I'm pretty sure he only made contact because I had mentioned the lack of contact in my feedback. I had specifically mentioned that I had not heard from him despite the promise made by the service desk.

Another incident occurred at the cocktail testing. I love this kind of event as it is easy for me to participate; it cost $35 each to attend. This time, because of Keegan we were placed in a corner away from the main seating area around a table where all the action was happening. Despite my low vision making it hard to see, I do usually enjoy hearing the banter that goes along with how the cocktails are made. Despite being put it the corner, we did get to taste everything, and I felt we received value for money.

After the tasting finished, the guest service manager, Duncan, approached me. He came to seek me out because he received the complaints I had made via the cruise company's feedback app. He promised to remind all staff of Guide Dog etiquette and assured me that I could contact him anytime via a special app. It was not an app I had installed on my phone. When he learnt I had paid for internet access on board the ship, he offered to refund my money for internet usage so that I could contact him at any time. This was his way of apologising.

As I was sitting in the cabin that evening, the phone rang. I got up and answered; a male voice on the other end announced that he was from the medical clinic and wanted to speak to Janice. I was concerned about why he was calling me as the first thing that came to mind was COVID. He insisted that I needed to come to Deck 4, where the clinic was located, and speak in front of all medical staff, explaining how I lost my sight, how it had affected me and how Keegan makes my life easier. All of the medical staff wanted to learn. I felt very uncomfortable with this request.

I demanded to know exactly who he was and how he got my details. It turned out he was the Chief Medical Officer and had received my details from Duncan. Feeling gobsmacked, I could not understand how they dared summon me, a paying passenger, to provide an educational talk on a matter that is not only extremely personal but sensitive. I hung up on him!

On Monday, 6 November 2023, we made our way to meet staff and other guests for our 8 a.m. meet and greet ahead of our pre-booked 8:30 a.m. 'Behind the Scenes' tour ahead of the Melbourne Cup. As the ship was running late to dock in Melbourne the meeting was postponed until 10 a.m.

I used the extra time to go to the guest services desk as I wanted to speak to Duncan about the disturbing phone call I received from the medical clinic. After waiting in line, I was eventually next in line. When it was my turn to be served, the female staff member decided to serve someone else and ignored me even though I was first.

"Fuck this, I've had enough!" My loud statement could be heard by everyone standing in the line as I stormed off. I walked around until I found a staff member who worked in one of the restaurants. I asked him if he could contact Duncan. This nice young man contacted his manager, who came over, spoke to me and assured me he'd been in contact with Duncan who was on his way down to see me. They got a chair for me to sit on.

A fellow cruise guest approached me "Hi Janice, it's Steven, we were talking earlier about the way I saw them treat you yesterday. They will sort it out eventually. Try and think positive". I responded that I wanted off the ship as I had been treated like shit from the moment I arrived at the port in Sydney.

Duncan arrived, and I told him about the refusal of service at the guest service desk and the uncomfortable phone call I had received. He seemed genuinely shocked about the phone call. I asked how the medical centre would know about me, including my name and cabin number.

"I wrote a letter to the entire ship's company reminding them of Guide Dog etiquette including your name and cabin number."

"So, you have breached my privacy!" I was furious; I let him know in no uncertain terms that I felt constantly discriminated against, and now breaching my privacy was the last straw.

Duncan assured me he would speak to the medical officer and that no harm had been intended. He also stated that he would contact the Captain and Head Office about my concern. After promising to get back to me soon, he left. I never saw or heard from him again. Nor did I hear from Head Office or the Captain.

It is not that I would have minded sharing how Keegan helps me; I am normally comfortable talking about the unique partnership that I share with Keegan. What had affronted me was the lack of sensitivity in asking me to talk about how I lost my sight, the tone in which the request was delivered, and most of all, the fact that I was on holiday and my privacy had been breached.

Given my earlier life, the abuse and encounters experienced at the hands of so-called medical professionals, all of which are detailed in my first book, my horrified reaction is not surprising.

By this time, we need to get back for our "Behind the Scenes" tour of the Melbourne Cup. On arrival at the meeting point we discovered they had changed the location. We rushed to the new location and scrambled aboard the bus with Keegan. We had paid a ridiculous $449.99 to attend and it was only when we were already on the bus when we were told that because the ship was late in docking we would not get to see the Melbourne Cup Trophy; getting up close to the Trophy is the only reason I paid for the tour. The tour was boring and unsatisfactory on multiple levels besides not getting to hold the Melbourne Cup we missed out on getting the lunch that has been advertised because the cruise ship was 2 hours late. Instead, we were served snacks. I was bitterly disappointed as I had wasted $899.98; I had to pay for my support worker to go with me.

By Thursday 9th November 2023 I still had not heard a peep from Duncan and not had the promised refund for internet usage materialised nor had there been any reserved seating for the entertainment show as promised.

That night, on returning to my cabin, there was a letter on my bed providing details of disembarkation times and location. There no information in regard to Keegan being checked by Biosecurity. I knew from past experiences that the cruise line always provides information on when and where I need to meet Biosecurity to have Keegan checked.

The next morning, because there was no information regarding Keegan and Biosecurity, I joined the massive queue waiting to disembark. We stood for 2 hours waiting for disembarkation. At 8:15 a.m., I was approached by a member of security who took me downstairs to a room to see Biosecurity. After taking a photo of Keegan, they said we could go. Keegan was not touched or checked for any fleas, ticks, soil etc. This was highly unusual and not what I was used to. I had to find my own way back into the main queue, because the security guard who had promised to take me back had vanished. Thankfully, Keegan was able to backtrack by following his own scent, to the ridiculously long queue. At approximately 9:20 a.m we finally disembarked the cruise ship even though our paperwork stated 7:20 a.m disembarkation.

As my foot touched solid ground I breathed a huge sigh of relief; the ordeal was over! I was off the cruise ship and back on shore; we found friendly service from the staff in the port terminal which made a refreshing change after what felt like an interminably long voyage.

Having heard nothing from the cruise company by 23 November 2023, despite my complaint in writing and numerous telephone calls, I found myself with no option but to turn to the Human Rights Commission. I lodged a formal complaint against that cruise company and have vowed never to travel with them again. I do not wish this experience on anyone. Lodging the complaint is my way of hopefully bringing the company's attention to the fact that they need to look seriously at their training and communications across all levels. The situation with this liner began from the moment I stepped on board. As a paying passenger, I felt totally humiliated and discriminated against on so many levels.

###

Hamilton Island in the Whitsundays has always appealed to me. Palm trees, white sand, pristine waters, and luxury accommodation sounds like paradise, which is why I chose to treat myself to a trip of a lifetime. The trip was going to be my reward for completing the Cowell Challenge of 100 different parkruns.

Booking through Virgin in June 2022, I was surprised when asked if I had permission to take Keegan onto the island.

"What are you talking about? He's a Guide Dog and can go anywhere."

Reservations explained that I needed to call security on the island and let them know of my visit. The number provided by Virgin Reservations was answered by helpful security personnel. When I asked why they needed the information, the officer patiently clarified that although registered guide, hearing and assistance dogs are allowed, no other dogs are. To ensure that visitors have a smooth experience without any trouble, island security keeps a record of the dates of arrival and departure; these dates are then provided to all businesses on the island. The notification that a Guide Dog will be on the island ensures that the dog and handlers' presence will be respected, not questioned, refused entry, or distracted.

Impressed by the thoughtfulness, I once again telephoned Virgin; this time to confirm my booking including giving them the notice that I had followed instructions and notified the island security.

Our flight and check-in went smoothly. The following day, after participating in a parkrun, we ventured to Reef World by ferry for a unique night of underwater lodging at the Great Barrier Reef. The cost for this extraordinary experience was $1000 for the night. I realise it may sound extravagant, but it was a rare opportunity, and, on this occasion, I decided to splash out instead of being on my usual strict budget.

The underwater accommodation was truly spectacular. Our room with a transparent wall looking out into the colourful marine life, filled me with a sense of wonder and excitement. The night was spent drifting off to sleep with the soothing sound of the ocean making me feel truly at one with nature.

Waking up to the first light filtering through the water was a surreal experience. It was a humbling reminder of the importance of preserving our oceans and the need to protect these precious environments.

As Keegan and I made our way back to the mainland, I felt grateful for having had the chance to experience such a unique and unforgettable adventure. The memories created during our night at the Great Barrier Reef will forever hold a special place in my heart, reminding me of the magic that awaits us when we are willing to step out of our comfort zone and embrace the wonders of the world.

###

Kindness comes from the most unexpected quarters and one thing I have learnt is that you can never tell how people will react and that I must never judge or assume.

Riverfire, an event held annually in Brisbane, is something that has been on my wish list for several years. I finally decided to go in September last year (2023). Given that more than 500,000 people typical attend the event, I knew it would be a challenge trying to navigate despite having Keegan to guide me.

I finally decided that a boat cruise would be the best way to attend, and even though the company did not offer reserve seating, when I told them that I had a Guide Dog, they allocated us a table.

When we embarked on the cruise, we were led to our table which was near to the band. Just as we sat down, a crew member approached me.

"We'd like to move you."

"Why?" I was suspicious.

"We think you'll be more comfortable if you follow me; I'll show you where we think will be better. If you don't like it, you can come back here." Concerned that being so close to the live band would be detrimental to Keegan, I followed.

On the next deck, I was introduced to the captain, who greeted me warmly. "I heard a Guide Dog was on board, and I think you'll enjoy being up here." He invited us to stay on the private deck, which had access to the internal cabin and a private toilet. It was the most perfect spot. We could hear the music without our eardrums being blasted to pieces.

As the fireworks show began, the collective gasps from the crowd and kaleidoscope of colours that I could dimly make out – my vision is extremely limited, and I only see a blur – sent shivers of delight up my spine. Even though I could not clearly see what I knew were stunning displays of incredible artistic design, especially the Spirit of the Whale, which told the story of the indigenous ledge about the creation of Moreton Bay islands, I was having a fantastic time soaking up the atmosphere of the balmy night.

When the evening ended, the captain gave me his personal phone number and instructed me to call him if I decided to book a cruise to Moreton Island on their vessel. He assured me he would make sure he was rostered on so Keegan and I would once again be able to join him on deck away from the crowds.

It was a brilliant evening made all the more special by the kindness of the captain of Micat – the iconic Brisbane Ferry that runs regularly to Moreton Island. The magic of Riverfire will be etched on my memory forever.

"We need to make every single thing accessible to every single person with a disability."

Stevie Wonder

Food, Wine & Events

I love living adventurously! For too long, I was restricted. Now, given my limited abilities to cook for myself, I am seizing the opportunity by attending events, visiting wineries, and enjoying different foodie experiences.

If you are wondering why a legally blind individual like me would want to go out so much, the answer is that we need to escape the four walls we live in. It is a personal choice of how we identify ourselves.

I choose to identify as being up for fun! I do not allow my disability to stop me from seeking opportunities to experience culture, travel and adventure, although how I do that has changed since Keegan became a part of my life.

In May 2022, I wanted to attend a performance at a major centre in Brisbane. They did not discriminate against Keegan's attendance, but they required him to sit on my lap throughout the show.

This totally goes against the rule of 'All paws on the floor', destroys the two years of training, and would make both Keegan and me extremely uncomfortable within five minutes.

I did not purchase the ticket as the rules were not realistic.

####

On Christmas Eve, Sunday 24 December 2023, whilst visiting Dromana in Victoria, I decided to visit a rum distillery in between the two parkruns that I was there to do. A male and female staff member greeted me at the door saying that I was welcome to sit outside with my dog.

I explained Keegan, as a working Guide Dog, was legally allowed to enter the distillery. They were insistent we had to be outside and went so far as to suggest we sit at the table closest to the inside area. Our discussion got a little bit louder as they were refusing to listen.

"I will be filing a complaint," were my parting words as I turned to leave.

A woman approached me, saying, "You and your guide dog are welcome to sit anywhere you like".

"Are you the manager?" After confirming that she was, I instructed Keegan to find a table.

I ordered a sampler, which is 4 small pots of their rum and a meal. As I was eating, the male staff member who kept refusing me access came up to the table.

"My sister has a guide dog and gets refused entry all the time." I instantly thought, 'Is he stupid or what?' 'Was he being sarcastic?'.

"Well, you should know better then!" I snapped at him.

I finished my meal and rum samples and vowed never to return. The manager was fine but the 2 staff at the door were ignorant. However, it was the comment from the male staff saying his sister has a guide dog that really pissed me off.

####

One of the funniest incidents took place when I was wait-ing for breakfast at a cafe in Mango Hill after completing a parkrun.

Keegan knows the place well, as we frequently go there. After leading me to our usual table, I sat down as he settled under my chair.

Two ladies were dining separately inside the cafe. One sat at 9 o'clock, and the other at 1 o'clock. The three of us struck up a conversation, randomly chatting about parkrun and Keegan. The lady sitting at 1 o'clock shared that she was the mother of two of the young staff members and was waiting to pick them up after their shift.

Shortly after, a staff member came over. "We have tables outside that you can sit at."

I responded, "It's fine, we'll stay inside where the aircon is, thanks."

"Your dog can't be inside," she replied.

"He is a Guide Dog," I retorted. "He is in uniform, and he is legally allowed inside." She gave me 'that look.'

"The Guide Dog is allowed in here; leave her alone". The lady sitting at 1 o'clock jumped to my defence.

The staff member walked off. "I've gotten so used to this that it's a joke!" I said to the lady.

My new friend at the next table turned to me, saying, "Wait till I get her home!"

It turns out the waitress was her daughter. I don't think she'll make the same mistake again. I can guarantee that when

Mum took her daughters home, there would be some form of lecturing going on. Keegan and I have been going to this particular cafe for 3 years. It just shows that training is something the establishment lacks when it comes to new staff.

Genuine mistakes are totally acceptable. Young staff cannot be expected to know if they are not taught during their induction. My personal thoughts are that it should not be rocket science. As part of any on the job training, along with washing hands, food hygiene etc, it should be included that a Guide Dog is legally allowed entry – but not into the food preparation areas.

It's important to understand that a guide, hearing or assistance dog is not a pet or a 'companion' dog. The *Guide, Hearing and Assistance Dogs Act 2009* (the Act) came into effect on 1 July 2009.

The important piece of legislation states that handlers and their certified dog have access rights to public places e.g restaurants and shops, public passenger vehicles that includes trains or taxis as well as accommodation such as hotels and campgrounds.

In a nutshell, it is unlawful to discriminate by refusing entry or access to a public place because a person relies on a guide, hearing or assistance dog.

Funnily, a couple of weeks ago at the parkrun, a woman approached me and introduced herself as the person sitting at the 9 o'clock position at the cafe where the kid waitress had tried to refuse me entry. Keegan and I made such an impression that she had decided to start doing parkrun herself.

\#\#\#\#

I manage a regular social group with over 2ooo members. For something different, I arranged to meet at an Indian restaurant in Mango Hill. There were about twenty attending, and it was a place I had not been before. As is my habit, I stay at the end of the table. Being on the end makes it easier for Keegan to be out of the way under my chair and not hindering anyone else.

The man from behind the counter came up. "You'll have to leave," he said politely. When I explained Keegan was a Guide Dog, he continued, "We can't have a dog in here because if the Council sees, they will fine us about $2,000".

"You'll be likely to get a fine of about $60,000 if you kick me out." I left and put up a post about being refused entry. A member of the public saw my post and contacted the restaurant expressing outrage at how wrong they had been to refuse me entry.

The next thing I knew, the restaurant owner messaged me, saying they genuinely did not know a Guide Dog was permitted in a restaurant. He was genuinely appalled to hear they had broken the law and discriminated against me.

"Next time you come with your group, dinner will be on us. On the house for everyone."

Believing in his sincerity and willingness to make things right, I arranged another social outing to the restaurant. We had a lovely evening with delicious food and excellent service.

I deliberately chose not to inform the group that their meals were complimentary to prevent anyone from exploiting the situation by ordering the most expensive meals, wines and spirits. Everyone placed their orders as usual.

I ordered what I would normally choose if I were paying my own bill and a bottle of wine. I didn't want to take advantage. There is no need to be greedy. Savouring our meals, engaging in lively conversation, and being in the moment was heartwarming. I love going out for a meal with friends, it's a highlight in my calendar given that most evenings I spend alone at home with Keegan.

One of the ladies had to leave early, so she went to the counter to pay. "It's on the house. Janice is covering the bill," smiled the cashier. It was her first time attending one of the outings that I ran, and needless to say, her reaction was one of delighted incredulity.

Only as the evening wound down, when it was time to leave, and everyone in the group was asking for their bill, did I share that the meals and drinks were on the house as an apology for their earlier treatment of myself and Keegan.

No one paid a penny, or perhaps the correct term should be no one paid a cent. It was the restaurant's way of saying, "We are sorry." I appreciated the efforts and expense that management had gone to in order to correct a mistake they had made.

The evening ended on a high note. Gratified to know that the restaurant was genuinely sorry, I knew this was now a place I could return to again with no fear of being denied entry. True apologies and genuine hospitality lie not in flawless service but in how a venue handles hiccups and turns them into opportunities to show care and generosity.

####

Earlier this year (2024), I decided to visit wineries near Singleton during my visit to the Newcastle Hunter region. At the first two, I was instantly asked to take my dog outside, as dogs were not allowed inside. Each time, I had to educate them that Keegan was not a pet but a registered Guide Dog. I sometimes think I need an auto-start button that plays a recording given the amount of time I have to spend repeating the same message about Guide Dogs.

At my third stop, I struck it lucky. Honey Wines Australia Meadery gave Keegan and me a warm welcome; we were made to feel like valued visitors. These people obviously knew how to run a business and the laws around Guide Dogs, which was a refreshing change from the reception I had received at the previous wineries. The visit was a highlight of our trip, and their mead was awesome. I ended up spending $450 and have no hesitation in recommending the place.

As usual, I often share my adventures and experiences through social media. It plays a significant role in my life by connecting me to the outside world. Facebook helps me feel less isolated and lonely. While I know and fully accept the drawbacks, the connections are valuable to me.

With every post I share, I feel a sense of community and belonging that breaks down the physical boundaries. It's surprising how a few taps on the keyboard and a simple button click spark conversations, laughter, and comfort from friends and supporters. Despite the occasional negativity that can seep through, I hold onto the positive connections and shared experiences that make social media a valuable part of my life. The digital connection reminds me that I am never truly alone in a world that can sometimes feel vast, lonely, and daunting.

Triple M radio station contacted me the day after my post went up. One of my followers had shared that I had been refused entry by two wineries in the Newcastle region. It struck my followers as strange that a place known for tourism would not know the rules around the rights of admission for a Guide Dog.

As I spoke with the radio hosts, I shared my experience and highlighted the importance of raising awareness about accessibility for people with disabilities. The radio interview sparked a public discussion on social media, with many people sharing their own experiences and showing support for making all public places inclusive and welcoming.

Bren Barber, one of my followers, posted, "You have got people talking about the Guide and assistance dog discrimination issue in the Newcastle region today. I was at two medical appointments today, and in both waiting rooms, people were discussing your interview this morning on the Triple M Breakfast show - Newcastle. It's so wonderful that people now have a greater understanding of the challenges visually impaired people face on a regular basis and are openly having discussions about the issue, as they can help those being discriminated against & educate those naive people who are not educated on the legal rights."

To be fair, I must share that I have visited some great venues where Keegan is never a problem. One common thing to most of these venues is that they are all part of Australian Venue Co.

This company deserves a shout-out for whatever training they are running - it is effective!

If you are curious, here's the list of the establishments that I have visited with Keegan and had absolutely no trouble whatsoever.

VIC - Fargo & Co,

WA - The Bassendean Hotel, Dirty Nelly's Irish Pub, The Claremont Hotel, Wolf Lane

NT - Shenanigans

SA - Mile End Hotel

QLD - Brighton Hotel, Hotel Allen, Jubilee Tavern, Woodpecker Bar & Grill, Waterloo Hotel, Wallaby Hotel, Tom's Tavern, Sundowner Hotel Motel, Redcliffe Tavern, Morayfield Tavern, Mango Hill Tavern, The Local Tavern, Finnegan's Chin Keperra, Jindalee Hotel, Diamonds Kallangur, Ferry Road Tavern, Everton Park Hotel, Bribie Island Hotel, Berserker Tavern, Beenleigh Tavern.

As you can see from the above list it covers five States and a Territory. This cannot be a coincidence and goes to suggest that management are proactive in their approach to staff training.

On the flips side of my experiences with Australian Venue Company establishments is a franchise chain of cafes whose menu I absolutely adore and always choose to frequent whenever I finish a parkrun if there is one in the local vicinity.

It's called Café 63 which originally started at #63 Racecourse Road, Brisbane. Today there are over 50 of these cafes at various locations including interstate. It is one of my favourite places to go for brunch after a parkrun. The menu caters for my dietary requirements in the sense that I can build my own brunch.

My local Café 63 in Morayfield is wonderful, and there is never a problem with a refusal. Sadly, the same cannot be said for Café 63 Coomera, Redcliffe, Smith Collective, Eastville and Ross Evans Garden Centre, which is a real shame.

I attended Paradise Point parkrun on 12 March 2022 and after completing our 5km run went to Westfield Coomera to have breakfast at Café 63 Coomera. After finding a table and just as we were ready to place our order a staff member approached me telling me that I must leave as dogs are not allowed into the cafe. I informed her that Keegan is a registered Guide Dog, and legally allowed into the cafe. She disagreed and insisted that I had to leave. I asked to speak to the manager after which I was allowed to stay. I had a quick breakfast as the staff made me feel uncomfortable.

I made contact with the head office of Café 63 on Wednesday 16 March to lodge a complaint and received a response from Hamish Watson on March 17, 2022. His response was that he would send a reminder to all franchisees to be mindful of the law regarding Guide Dog access. I later discovered that Hamish was the founder and owner of the Café 63 brand.

On Friday, April 1, 2022, upon arrival at Redcliffe Café 63, no sooner had I sat down when a female staff member came up to tell me that I must go and sit outside as dogs are not allowed in the cafe. We pointed to the wall informing her that there was a sign in black and white stating that guide and assistance dogs are welcome. She responded, "Oh, I didn't know." We had our breakfast and then left.

Wednesday, April 6th, 2022, I sent a message to Hamish Watson on the 6 April letting him that what had occurred and informing him I would be filing a formal complaint with the Human Rights Commission. An hour later, I received a message that someone called Barbara would be in touch to discuss my issue.

Barbara made contact via telephone and gave me a guarantee that all staff would be reminded that Guide Dogs are allowed inside the café.

Saturday 4th March 2023, after completing the 5km parkrun at Kingscliff, we went to Café 63 Smith Collective and as we approached the entrance were asked if we would like a table outside. After stating a preference to be inside we were shown to a table. As we sat discussing the menu I was approached for identification; I produced the GHAD identification card.

"You need to sit up the back," the server handed back my card and pointed to the other end of the cafe.

I asked why to which came the response, "Because the kitchen is over there." The kitchen was in a different room so I pointed out that I could not be forced to sit up at the back because I have a Guide Dog.

"I'm just doing what I'm told," came the response when I told her about the GHAD laws. Again, she repeated, "I'm just doing what I'm told."

It was an 'out of sight, out of mind' situation. I told her that I did not have to move; this is where we were seated, and we were staying right there. She insisted that the manager had instructed her to move us to the other end of the cafe, claiming we were too close to the kitchen. I dug my heels in and repeated that we did not have to move as we were sitting at a table in the dining area. She refused to serve us, so we had no choice but to leave. We were in and out in 9 minutes.

We googled for the nearest Café 63 and found Café 63 Ross Evans which is located within a nursery. When we approached the counter for seating, the female staff told us that we needed to sit in the dog friendly area. I explained that Keegan was wearing his harness and is a working Guide Dog. She apologised and offered to seat us at table 100 in the regular area.

After being discriminated against at four separate venues within the franchise because of having a Guide Dog, I messaged Hamish at the head office again. Disappointing, there was no response which speaks volumes; I decided to file a case with the Australian Human Rights Commission. I decided to go to the national body rather than the Queensland body as the franchisee operates in multiple States.

The day after the National Hotel incident, I went to Eastville Café 63 for breakfast. If you are thinking "she is nuts going there", the reason is that I must be careful to follow my Keto diet to aid with controlling my epilepsy. There are very few places where I can create my own menu at a reasonable price. When I whipped out my phone to record the refusal by three of their staff members the manager noticed what was happening, came over to sort out the problem and I was allowed to stay. It is abundantly clear that Hamish, despite being the owner and therefore well positioned to take action, did not keep his promise to train or inform staff in regard to assistance dogs.

A conciliation hearing was set for 15 February 2024. It took over 12 months to get to the point where a date was set. 3 days prior to the hearing, I received a call from the HRC advising me that Café 63 was not prepared to attend conciliation or even prepared to offer any apologies for the refusals.

Despite it not being my original intention to name and shame in this book, I feel strongly that their unwillingness to address the discrimination against Keegan and myself warrants Café 63 Australia being named. It is my hope that public pressure might be brought to bear so that change will happen within this franchise. The fact that the national office which sets the standards is unwilling to address this issue is shameful.

####

One of my support workers took me to the Hellfire Club. I had never been to this Club before but had heard about it and decided to go along as I am always up for a new adventure.

I felt more than a teeny bit nervous as she dropped me off outside the venue and left me with Keegan on the pavement as she parked the car. The security guard on duty offered to get me a chair to sit in while I waited. As I sat there, I couldn't help but feel a sense of excitement building up inside me.

As we entered the dimly lit club, the sounds of pulsating music filled my ears. I could make out faint shadowy shapes, which my support worker explained were suitcases. Almost everyone had one - everyone except us.

No one batted an eyelid at Keegan. A big, burly guy dressed in leathers sauntered up.

"Madam, I am here to serve your dog". He took up a position standing in front of Keegan. "My master told me to serve your dog."

A woman asked if Keegan would like a bowl of water. Keegan was accepted and, apart from the offer of water, was ignored as a Guide Dog should be.

As the evening went on, the suitcases opened to reveal they contained cattle prods! Throughout the night, people kept coming over to ask me if I would like to try the prod.

In my travels, I have noticed that minority communities generally accept Keegan and myself more. Less discrimination occurs in these kinds of places regardless of where I am in Australia. It has occurred to me that this may be because they are more aware of discrimination since they are often on the receiving end.

"There's more to sight than meets the eye, and I am capable of seeing it all."
Janice Whittle

Refusals in Least Expected Spots

"Get your fucking dirty hands off our meat!" bellowed the voice across the butchery section.

I stood rooted to the spot in shock! With Keegan by my side, I'd picked up a pack of meat and was holding it up close trying to make out the price tag.

The butchery assistant of a major Australian supermarket had immediately judged me based on appearance; could they not see I had a Guide Dog? Recovering my composure, I asked to speak to the manager. This was a classic case of prejudice based on my appearance.

I received an apology and the promise this would not happen again, but I was visibly shaken. This experience added to the many that have led me to become an online shopper. I choose to subscribe and pay for unlimited deliveries so I do not have to run the risk of abuse. People say I am isolating myself, but for me, it feels safer and is easier than facing discrimination at all levels, including finding transport on what should be a simple trip to the supermarket.

The same supermarket allows assistance animals into its

premises, including ones that sit in trolleys. When questioned about their policy regarding verification of the animal's right to be in the supermarket, they answered that they would ask the individual for identification for the assistance dog but not the individual's disability (as it should be).

I then asked what they do if someone refuses or cannot provide identification. The response shocked me. The spokesperson said the policy is then to ask the handler to prove the dog can obey simple commands, such as telling the dog to sit. If the dog sits, they accept that as evidence that it is an assistance dog.

Another large supermarket gave a similar answer: They would not ask for proof that the animal was an assistance animal in case the handler became offended; their priority is to protect their staff from abuse. To say this annoys me immensely is an understatement.

We have laws in place to protect our rights and the rights of all shoppers. And yet major supermarkets are afraid to enforce them for fear of offending shoppers who, in most cases, do not have a certified assistance animal that has passed the Public Access Test. This is a major problem.

On the flip side of this coin, those of us who do have all the necessary legal paperwork are being discriminated against on a regular basis. In my opinion, these so-called "assistance" animals are giving a bad name to certified assistance animals like Keegan and other Guide Dogs.

\#\#\#\#

In September 2021, I had sold my house in Toowoomba and was actively looking to purchase another property. There was a house advertised that I was keen to view, so I followed all the real estate instructions and registered to attend the open house. The registration process includes providing name and contact details.

When I arrived for the open inspection, the real estate agent at the door barred me from entering on the basis that no dogs were allowed. Despite my explanation of the law, and the fact that an open inspection made the house a public place for those particular hours, I was still refused entry.

Later that afternoon, I received a phone call from the real estate office asking if I had a Guide Dog. I do not know what process of elimination they went through of all the prospective buyers to identify me, but it was clear they had gone to some lengths to track me down once they had realised that I should not have been refused entry.

The chap on the phone explained that in all the years of showing houses they had never had a situation where someone with a Guide Dog had turned up to inspect. He was extremely apologetic and asked if I would be interested in a 1:1 inspection that afternoon. I accepted the offer as he was genuine, and I did want to see the house. I did not end up buying that property, but I do believe at least that agency and staff were enlightened by my visit and now know the rights of a Guide Dog when it comes to holding open inspections of houses for sale.

####

On 26th October 2022, I walked to my local branch of a national hardware and homewares store. Eager to work on my garden, I planned to buy supplies for creating a home-grown vegetable garden in my new home, but unfortunately, I was turned down for service twice!

This was different in the sense that I was not refused entry. It was a staff member who did not want to serve someone who had a disability.

"Excuse me." I could make out a staff member standing in front of us. I wanted to ask for directions to the right section of the mammoth size store, but she looked at me with filth before walking off.

Feeling taken aback by her reaction, Keegan and I stood there frozen, rooted to the spot for a few moments before moving on to try and find the products independently. About 10 minutes later, the same staff member walked towards me from the opposite direction. Again, I asked for assistance; Keegan and I were standing right next to her when I asked, but again, she looked directly at me, pulled a face, and walked off as if she had never been there.

Yep, I was refused service on two separate occasions by the same staff member. This was not a case of guide dog refusal, as the store allows all customers to bring their pets (personally, I don't like it, but that is their policy), but it was a case of blatantly refusing to serve a customer with a disability. She saw that I had a guide dog and decided to make faces at me while refusing to acknowledge me and provide service.

I guess this staff member did not realise that I do have a level of vision and was able to see her 'body language'. I left without making a purchase but on the way out, I spoke to management, but I believe I wasted my time. This was the last place I ever expected to receive such blatant discrimination.

####

In August 2023, I attended the Moreton Bay Food and Wine Festival, where Miguel Maestre from The Living Room was hosting a 3-course Spanish feast. I loved the food while I was in Spain, so it was a no-brainer to sign up for this special feast.

The occasion was fabulous! Keegan and I had a friendly chat and a photo taken with Miguel; I thoroughly enjoyed every moment of the experience.

The next day, I had booked to attend a seafood buffet lunch, and it, too, was magnificent and memorable for all the right reasons.

Day three was dinner with Ladies Who Long Lunch. I loved the sound of the name, and the event's promotion had me convinced it would be a wonderful, fun event in great company. How wrong I was. The trouble started from the moment I arrived. They were not impressed that I had a Guide Dog. The reception I received on arrival was totally at odds with my experiences at the previous two events, which I had thoroughly enjoyed.

I was told that Keegan would have to sit outside the 'tent' and pointedly moved to a spot where my seat was pushing up against a tent pole, with Keegan outside in the rain. I left within 5 minutes as it was obvious I was not welcome, and the event organiser made it plain that they had no intention of accepting or catering to my disability. I was unwelcome. They might not have actually gone so far as to say that, but it was clear from the attitude towards me.

After complaining to the festival management, I was re-funded the $139 for the dinner and received an apology for the staff attitude of Ladies Who Long Lunch.

One of the major issues of contention which makes it more difficult for those with genuine assistance animals is what I call "fake" assistance dogs. Harnesses are available on-line with whatever anyone might choose to have printed on them. By contrast, a genuine Guide Dog who is working is always seen wearing an official issue harness as opposed to a simple leash and jacket. The only Guide Dogs you will ever see in a jacket are those that are currently in training.

"Fake" assistance animals are often seen being carried, sitting in laps, even eating alongside their handler and worst yet, with their paws on the table! These animals and handlers do not have the same level of training, nor do they have the identity documents that both Keegan and I carry attesting to our certification.

Sadly, many establishments are afraid to challenge the "handlers" for fear of repercussions like a public scene. Fear of a public scene is no excuse for not seeking appropriate identification.

####

It seems that even Santa is not immune to discrimination. Last December, on Friday 22, 2023 to be precise, I was in a large shopping centre in Victoria when I decided it would be rather nice to have a photo of Keegan and myself with Santa.

"What do you want?" snarled Santa as Keegan and I approached. Not quite the jolly Santa greeting I anticipated.

"To have our photo taken, please." I put on my best smile for Santa and his Elf.

"We don't allow photos with pets in case a child has an allergy to dog hair" responded Santa.

"You can obviously see that he is not a pet," I indicated to Keegan's harness, "He is a Guide Dog".

"I don't care," came the very un-Santa like response, "No pets allowed. Pets aren't allowed in the Plaza. You should leave"

"I will be lodging a complaint" I retorted before walking away.

I posted publicly on my page regarding my discriminating experience and tagged the shopping centre in the post. The majority of my followers expressed shock at the experience; some commented sympathetically, and a few even went as far as tagging the centre which I had named.

One of my social media followers, Tanya Messell, messaged my Facebook page, *Janice's Vision of Life* sharing that she had received a personal Facebook Message from the Centre.

"Dear Tanya,

Thank you for bringing this matter to our attention. We understand your concern about the situation that occurred with the service dog and Santa at the photography set.

Ensuring the safety and comfort of everyone is our top priority, and this includes maintaining a hygienic environment for children and individuals with allergies. Following specific pet photography hours is a carefully considered protocol to minimise cross-contamination and potential discomfort.

However, we completely understand that service dogs are not pets and play a critical role in the lives of their owners. While our designated pet photography hours offer a controlled environment for other animals, turning away a service dog outside of those times does not align with our values of inclusivity and accessibility.

We are immediately reviewing our policies and procedures to ensure that service dogs are welcomed at all times during our events, with appropriate measures in place to address any potential concerns for other guests.

We appreciate your feedback and for helping us identify this oversight. We are committed to learning from this experience and ensuring that such a situation does not occur again. If you have any further questions or concerns, please do not hesitate to contact us.

Warm regards"

To say that I was shocked that the Centre had privately messaged Tanya Messell but decided to have no contact with me is an understatement. Throughout our visit to the Centre, Keegan was in uniform, clearly saying Guide Dogs Australia on his harness. I proceeded with a complaint against the Centre as they did not seem genuinely apologetic due to the lack of direct contact with me.

####

Keegan and I, accompanied by my support worker Jenny, visited Morayfield Shopping Centre recently. While strolling through the air-conditioned centre, a man emerged with a Pitbull sporting a harness. The Velcro sign on the harness proudly displayed the words 'Service Dog'.

Straining against its leash, the Pitbull 'Service Dog' snarled and growled menacingly as it headed straight for Keegan. The male on the other end of the leash, sporting dark glasses, was holding onto the lead with all his strength, trying to control his 'service dog'. Thankfully, he managed to pull it away, and they walked off.

Despite being shaken by the incident, Keegan managed to compose himself and resume his work after receiving re-assurance from me. Shaken to the core at our close encounter, pictures flashed through my mind of the totally different outcome that might have occurred had the male not been able to hold his dog back. Anyone can buy a harness and service or assistance dog signs on eBay, but it does not make your dog a legitimate assistance dog.

Guide, Hearing and Assistance Dogs are trained for very

good reasons. Therapy/emotional support/companion dogs are not recognised under the Guide, Hearing and Assistance Dogs Act 2009 as the owner may not have a disability and/or the dog has not been trained to undertake specific, identifiable tasks and behaviours to aid the person's disability.

The Guide, Hearing and Assistance Dogs Act 2009 protects these rights and imposes penalties for people and businesses breaching the legislation. For example, a person or business separating an approved handler or trainer with a certified dog from other patrons in any public area may be fined up to $12,190 for an individual, and $60,950 for a corporation.

This Act ensures that individuals who require the assistance of guide, hearing, or assistance dogs are able to access public spaces without discrimination. By imposing significant fines for violations, it emphasises the importance of respecting the rights of individuals who rely on these specially trained animals for support. This legislation serves as a reminder that inclusivity and accommodation for people with disabilities must be a top priority, promoting the message that a more accessible and compassionate community is a basic human right.

####

Short Term Accommodation (STA) is available as a break for most NDIS participants. There are specialised providers who cater especially to the disability sector.

In my case, registered STA providers were happy to accept my booking until I mentioned the word Guide Dog. Each of them stated they do not allow dogs. Considering they are disability-focused accommodations, it made no sense at all to me.

These are disability services refusing to provide service because I have a disability aid. It's just crazy, in fact, it's unbelievable. I left it for a few months, and after talking to my NDIS plan manager, decided to give it another go. Once again, every STA I spoke to refused to allow Keegan to be with me.

I totally gave up and then decided to arrange a self-designed STA. It was the best decision I made. A three-night (Fri, Sat & Sun) STA organised by the official provider will cost $7,923.55, but when I created a self-designed STA, the three nights cost approximately $1250.00. It is a massive saving, and I do not have to put up with the discrimination.

####

Spotting an event advertised on Facebook that was being run on 10 May 2023 by the RSPCA, I decided to attend. It was for all Centrelink pension card holders in the area with the focus being people and their pets. Even though Keegan is not actually a pet, I felt it would be beneficial for me to attend and see what I might learn. Plus, it was an outing for me. I booked my spot and made arrangements for a support worker to assist me on the day.

On arrival we approached the registration table and filled in the form. I was then directed to the next table where I was asking if I had any concerns about Keegan. At the following table they asked me about my living arrangements; because I had a home that table was not one where I needed to spend much time, so I move on to the next table.

The table was hosted by the Neighbourhood Centre. Their information interested me, and I remained there for quite some time having a chat about accessibility and Guide Dog refusals. The people looking after the stall were shocked to hear about my experiences and assured me that Keegan and I were welcome at any time as they explained about various classes at the centre including computer, cooking, parenting, relationships, budgeting, anger management etc. Handing me information pamphlets, I was encouraged to join in any group activities that appealed to me.

The next stop was a hydrobath for Keegan and then a checkup by the vet. Our final stop was with Pet Barn who handed out some secondhand dog toys and a bag of dog biscuits. It was a fun, informative outing, and I was glad that I made the effort to attend; I felt welcome, and that Keegan and I were accepted.

A few weeks later I received a call from the Neighbourhood Centre about a class I had put my name down for. She went very quiet when I said I would be bringing my Guide Dog.

"I will get back to you". She finally said before hanging up. There was a distinct change in her demeanour.

The next day, she rang back to apologetically explain that I could not bring Keegan to their centre as it was against their policy. I started to explain the laws and rights of a Guide Dog, but suddenly, overcome with weariness, I gave up. Depleted of energy, I was sick and tired of having to explain these laws every single day I leave the house. I have never had any further contact with that Neighbourhood Centre.

####

"Read the fucking sign, you stupid bitch. No dogs are allowed, so get the fuck out of here." These were the words directed at me when Keegan and I went to a National Park recently. The two men were leaving the park as we were about to enter. Keegan was in his Guide Dog harness but that did not stop them menacingly coming towards me as they pointed at the sign.

I answered that I understood the sign, but a Guide Dog was legally allowed and had identification, they still advanced towards us. I quickly backed away with my support worker.

When they eventually drove off, we entered the Park and had a good day walking around with Keegan in his harness by my side. Making our way to the café after our walk, I chatted to the manager and shared what had happened. This is not an uncommon incident. For me, it was a typical day in public with the abuse that Keegan and I face from the general community.

It's Not Rocket Science

An idea I came up with to help with education is to include information about Guide Dog access in the paperwork when a business applies for a food license or permit. The Council could incorporate this into the process, with a check box for applicants to acknowledge their awareness of the legislation. This would facilitate easier follow-up in case of complaints and serve as a reminder to businesses about their understanding and compliance.

All staff cannot be expected to know legislation if they are not taught the rules during their induction. I've noticed that some of the younger staff on working holiday visas to Australia are unaware of our laws.

My personal thoughts are that it should not be rocket science. The business owner is the responsible person, and in the hospitality industry, as part of any on-the-job training, along with washing hands, food hygiene, etc, it should be included that a Guide Dog is legally allowed entry – but not into the food preparation areas.

To further support business owners, I had the idea that staff education and compliance, regular reminders, and updates on topics such as hand washing, food hygiene, and

Guide Dog regulations could be sent out via email or displayed in the workplace on posters. The ongoing education would help reinforce good practices and ensure that all staff members are well-informed and equipped to handle various situations. It would also ensure compliance by owners and avoidance of hefty fines.

Investing in continuous education and training makes great business sense. It allows businesses to create a culture of awareness and responsibility among their staff which ultimately leads to a safer and more inclusive environment for everyone - both employees and customers.

Running regular training sessions specifically focused on these important topics would be hugely beneficial as they would provide an opportunity for staff to ask questions, clarify any doubts, and receive hands-on guidance. I even thought that perhaps someone who has a Guide Dog could be in attendance, which would ensure employees are more likely to retain crucial information and apply it effectively in real-life scenarios. Encouraging a culture of continuous learning and development not only benefits the employees but also contributes to the overall success and sustainability of the business as well as avoiding the risk of a hefty fine for failure to comply.

As a result of the discrimination I have faced, Keegan has a tracking tag on him at all times. What this means is that his exact locations and timing are recorded to make it more evident when he has been refused entry.

Google Maps records every movement I make and records the exact time of location, arrival and departure. The tag is further proof for when any of the discrimination cases go to court. It proves, without a shadow of a doubt, that he was by my side the entire time.

Another tool that I use is video recording glasses. I was asked if I was going to discuss these in this book given that I am often accused of trying to set people up so I can sue them. This could not be further from the truth.

The discrimination has reached the point where I need as much evidence as I can gather to prove that the discrimination is real. It is way too common.

Although my eyes fail me in being able to identify the person/people who have discriminated against Keegan and I, my 'artificial eyes' record everything. This tool makes it 100% possible to identify and hand all evidence to the courts.

Since Keegan came into my life, I have successfully settled thirteen cases. Six cases are currently waiting to be heard. Some of the companies are large household names and repeat offenders, including national supermarkets and transport and telecommunications giants; they are big guns.

These multinationals can be found in most shopping centres and on high streets ranging from major cities to small outback country towns; their products or services are used by the bulk of the Australian population, often on a daily basis. Their power, lawyers and tactics have been brought into play to try and scare me off.

In one of the cases that I pursued against a national transport carrier; the company had four lawyers lined up against me. To say that was intimidating is an understatement. It also demonstrates that they were worried, and to my mind, that is an admission of guilt if they needed to lawyer up so heavily against a blind woman and her dog.

I stood my ground despite feeling like they were attempting to bully me into submission and silence. Yes, I was quaking in my boots, but there was no way I could possibly accept what they were trying to intimidate me into agreeing to. It was morally and ethically wrong. I knew I had to stand up for what was right, not just for myself but for every other person who might face the same challenge in the future. When we stay silent, we are complicit.

The deal on the table that they were trying to coerce me into accepting included a substantial sum of cash. In return, I needed to agree to a lifetime gag and never again make a complaint against them. Given the fact that my complaint was genuine, obviously, so much so that they needed four lawyers to represent them, my answer was that if they were not prepared to be reasonable, I would go to the media. The case was settled.

In one case against a telecommunications giant, a settlement was made prior to conciliation as the situation occurred with a franchisee-owned outlet. The result was that the franchise was withdrawn. The discriminator is no longer in that business, and the company in question has ensured that all its franchisees are aware of the rights of Guide Dogs and their handlers.

My personal experience is that the larger the company, the more it is all about money. Putting profit before people means they have not invested in training beyond what has been the bare minimum. When priorities are solely focused on financial gains, the human aspect of the business tends to be neglected.

*"I'm tough, I'm ambitious, and I know exactly what I want.
If that makes me a bitch, okay."*

Madonna

Unconscious
Discrimination

Unconscious bias lurks in the shadows impacting how we interact with others and the choices we make. The actions of friends can often be hurtful. By creating awareness and actively challenging our own biases, we are each taking a significant step towards developing a more accepting and inclusive society. The fact you are reading this book is a testament to the fact that you are an enlightened part of the community that wants to make a difference.

There is a term "inspiration porn" which I heard for the first time recently, although when I delved further, I found it had been first used in 2012 when Australian comedian, journalist and disability rights activist Stella Young used it in an editorial in Australian Broadcasting Corporation's (ABC) webzine Ramp Up.

She also used the term in her TED Talk in 2014. The talk focused on how society objectifies people with disabilities as objects of inspiration. She pointed out that we often see images featuring an individual with a disability with text that reads: *The only disability in life is a bad attitude.*

Stella felt these images "objectify disabled people for the benefit of non-disabled people." She went on in her speech to say, "They are there so that you can look at them and think that things aren't so bad for you, to put your worries into perspective."

This term resonated deeply with me when I realised that what Stella meant is that society has such low expectations of disabled people that everyday activities, such as getting on the bus, are praised. These low expectations of disabled people like myself are often verbalised by those who are able-bodied with the best of intentions. People want to be inspired and recognise the hardships others have, but by doing so are perpetuating the label of being different.

Stella, in her talk, said: "I use the term porn deliberately because of the objectification of one group of people for the benefit of another group of people."

Whether you make assumptions based on someone's appearance or background, these biases can and do shape our interactions and decisions. It's unconscious bias because we are often not aware of it, nor do we fully comprehend what we are doing.

When you take the time to reflect on your own beliefs and attitudes, you start to understand the impact of your biases - and believe me, we all have them. It's part and parcel of being human. But what is important is for each of us to develop to the stage where we are willing to recognise this. It is only through our acknowledgement and awareness that we can then work towards creating a more equitable and open-minded approach to how we engage with those who may not conform to what we might consider societal norms.

From my first-hand experience, I know that by engaging in open conversations, actively seeking diverse perspectives, and consciously questioning my own preconceptions, I am able to start breaking down the barriers that unconscious bias creates. I wholeheartedly recognise and accept that this is a journey, and it is not an easy one.

To travel this journey, we need to be willing to examine what we have previously accepted as fact and to challenge our own self-awareness. During my years of abuse, I knew no different and accepted the world as it was presented to me. It was only when I began to emerge from the twilight zone that I gradually realised that embracing differences, questioning assumptions, and striving for understanding are crucial factors if we want to have a more inclusive and compassionate society.

I was at Mango Hill Tavern with a couple of friends for our usual Friday afternoon drinks and sausage sizzle. We always sit at one of the lower tables, allowing me to be closer to Keegan.

As we were sitting there having a drink and chatting, a male staff member approached my friend Steve.

"Does the Guide Dog want a drink?" he enquired kindly.

"How do I know? Ask Janice".

The staff member then asked Bob "Does her Guide Dog need a drink?"

Before Bob could respond, I snapped, "I am blind, not deaf! Keegan would love a drink."

This is what I call unconscious discrimination. People seem to think that being blind, you are unable to communicate in any way shape or form. This unconscious discrimination hurts me more than guide dog refusal.

####

Recently, while staying as a guest with friends, they wanted to go out for dinner. A friendly argument went on between the husband and wife for about 40 minutes on whether to go out for dinner or order a takeaway to avoid the chance of discrimination. Keegan and I were the problem. They didn't want the hassle of dealing with a refusal or to get involved in any kind of discrimination.

The argument and topic made me feel extremely uneasy. Sensing a heavy weight settling on my shoulders, I felt that I was a huge burden. Logically, I knew I was not a burden, but I could not help my feelings when faced with a topic that hit close to home.

I was the cause of the argument; the tension filling the room was palpable. Trying to maintain a sense of composure and restore balance, I spoke up, "You go out for dinner, and I'll stay here because I bought my own food anyway". I managed to keep my voice from shaking but my body language must have given away how uncomfortable they had made me feel.

Discrimination is everywhere - even in the people who think they are helping! My point is that these friends were unaware of the angst their actions were causing me. It was not their intention to make me feel uncomfortable; unconscious discrimination was at work. Gradually, the atmosphere lightened, a sense of understanding began to dawn, and they decided to go ahead and book a table.

To safeguard against trouble, they double-checked by contacting the restaurant an hour before our reservation to confirm that there would not be a problem once we arrived. To the immense relief of all of us, the restaurant reassured them that everything was in order with the booking. With a sense of reassurance that there was no cause for concern, we proceeded to get ready for our outing, looking forward to a pleasant evening ahead.

We rocked up to the venue where the staff member on duty at the door took one look at our party and immediately asked, "Would you like to sit outside?"

Exchanging glances with my friends, I replied without waiting for my friends to reply or skipping a beat.

"We'll sit inside, thanks."

The look of disdain was clear, but thankfully, that was as far as it went, nothing was actually said. We were led to an inside table and enjoyed an excellent meal.

Mum is often asked how people should act when I am around. Here's my advice: *Do not touch, talk, or look at me when I am working. Even when I am just lying there in harness, under a chair, I am still working.*

It's surprising how many individuals will address me, saying, *"I know I shouldn't talk to you; you're a Guide Dog, you're working, so I won't disturb you."* Yet, they end up looking directly at me and trying to get me into trouble by engaging in conversation.

The amount of people who talk to me rather than Mum

is seriously funny. It's like they think she is dumb as well as blind. I feel bad for Mum; she's either abused or ignored totally, and I am the star of the show. Seriously, Guide Dog etiquette dictates that you talk to the handler, that's Mum, and pretend I'm not there.

Honestly guys, it is best to just ignore a Guide Dog. As Mum says, *"You can think of the dog like a wheelchair. If you would not, touch, stare at, or ask about a person's wheelchair, then it's best to do the same for their Guide Dog."*

"Apologies are great, but they don't really change anything.
You know what does? Action."
Stella Young

Legislation

If you're speeding, being a total lunatic on the road, and almost killing people, there's a fine. A fine for speeding. There's a fine for dangerous driving. And when they pull you over and check your car "Oh, your lights aren't working. Your blinkers aren't working." There's a fine for that too.

Interestingly, a little-known fact is that the police have the power to issue a fine for refusing to take Guide Dogs and their handlers into vehicles or accepting them in a place that is accessible to the public. The key word is PUBLIC.

The term PUBLIC holds significance as it encompasses a wide range of areas where service animals should be welcomed without discrimination. It is essential for everyone to be aware of these regulations to promote a more inclusive and accommodating environment for those who rely on Guide Dogs for assistance. By upholding these guidelines, a more welcoming and supportive society is created for all members, including those with disabilities who depend on Guide Dogs like Keegan for their independence, physical, and mental well-being.

In my experience, it seems simpler to just warn the person responsible for discrimination and let them go with a minor reprimand. It's easier to say, "Don't do it again," to the discrimination offender and let them off with a slap on the wrist. It is not deemed as a serious enough offence which is why, on most occasions, I have personally given up contacting police.

It sounds like a cop-out (forgive the pun) when this book is about changing perceptions, but sometimes, willing up the energy, the willpower, and the courage to do battle is more than I can face some days.

In reality, addressing discrimination should never be dismissed lightly. While it may seem like a daunting task with paperwork and bureaucracy, it is crucial to stand up against any form of discrimination.

My advocacy for the rights of those with disabilities extends to trying to educate whenever I see misinformation. I am a member of a private camping group on social media, and the Moreton Bay City Council has just introduced new rules that dogs and cats are not allowed on the campsite.

One member thought claiming his pet dog as an assistance dog would be funny. I responded to his post saying that I did not find it amusing as so many people with fake assistance dogs cause an extraordinary amount of trouble for those of us who use a registered guide, hearing, or assistance dog. I felt hopeful that I had put my point across when the poster issued an apology.

By letting offenders off with just a warning, we are at fault, we are at fault because we are failing to work to create a safe and inclusive environment for everyone. It is important to report such incidents to the appropriate authorities, even if it feels like an uphill battle. Every report counts towards creating a more equal and just society. Our voices matter, and our actions can make a difference in combating discrimination. It is a slow process, but I truly do believe that change must eventually come.

I report offenders to GHAD, knowing that most of the time, they cannot do much except place their name on a list. If someone else experiences the same discrimination and reports it, the offenders cannot say they have not been warned.

I also make a point of reporting to the HRC, who are there to mediate. The HRC is not there to say, "You need to apologise to Janice. You need to refund her money because you wouldn't let her stay at the hotel, or you need to put your staff through training."

The response is often along the lines of "I know I did wrong, but I don't give a shit and you get nothing."

In those cases, the HRC come back to me saying it couldn't be settled. No one takes responsibility unless I want to pay for a solicitor and take someone to court, where the judge decides if I was discriminated against and what the outcome will be.

Rosemary Kayess, the Disability Discrimination Commissioner, has publicly stated that Australia's anti-discrimination measures need strengthening and reframing.

For anyone interested in looking further into the various pieces of legislation, that across Australia related to Guide Dogs, I have listed below the individual state laws. There is no Federal legislation, so it depends on each state.

In a 2022 Guide Dogs Queensland survey, over a third of members reported being refused service at least once over a 12-month period.

Queensland

Queensland is interesting as it was the first State to have specific legislation in Australia (1972) and the latest amendments came into effect 1st February 2024.

Guide Dogs Act 1972 (legislation.qld.gov.au) ORIGINAL ACT

Guide, Hearing and Assistance Dogs Act 2009 (legislation.qld.gov.au) AMENDED FEBRUARY 1ST 2024

Guide, Hearing and Assistance Dogs Act 2009 - Queensland Legislation - Queensland Government a link to all amendments

Western Australia

DOG ACT 1976 - SECT 8 (austlii.edu.au) WA

South Australia

DOG AND CAT MANAGEMENT ACT 1995 - SECT 81 (austlii.edu.au) SA

Tasmania

DOG CONTROL ACT 2000 (austlii.edu.au) TAS

New South Wales

COMPANION ANIMALS ACT 1998 - SECT 60 Assistance animal not to be denied entry (austlii.edu.au) NSW

Victoria

DOMESTIC ANIMALS ACT 1994 (austlii.edu.au) VIC
DOMESTIC ANIMALS ACT 1994 - SECT 7 Exemptions
for guide dogs (austlii.edu.au) VIC

"Acceptance doesn't mean resignation; it means understanding that something is what it is and that there's got to be a way through it."

Michael J. Fox

Being Mindful

Since Mum and I became a pair, we faced challenges and triumphs, learning and growing with each passing day. Whether it's guiding my human through busy streets, assisting with daily tasks, or simply being there as a source of comfort, I take pride in being by Mum's side and helping to change perceptions one guided step at a time. Our partnership goes beyond just being a Guide Dog and their handler - we are a team, a duo that complements each other in ways words cannot fully capture.

My favourite day of the week is Saturday because that's parkrun. It's the place where I know Mum is happiest because we are accepted and nobody makes a fuss about letting us join in. The kids are great too, and Mum teaches them they cannot talk to or touch me when I'm in my harness. But often, after the run is over, Mum removes my harness and slips me on the lead, which means I get to be fussed over big time. I love running around, playing with the kids and happily accepting the pats and attention that come my way.

As we continue to navigate life's ups and downs together, I am grateful for the opportunity to serve as a Guide Dog, not just for my Mum, but also as a beacon of hope and inspiration for all who witness the power of our bond. I am super proud of Mum who speaks up against all the injustice and discrimination she has faced since I came into her life.

You possibly have not thought of this, but common objects like cars parked across driveways, bins left out on footpaths, dumped bikes or scooters, and even people being distracted by mobile devices impact the freedom and independence of people with low vision or blindness.

Simple things like moving your bin off the footpath, not dumping bikes and scooters in public spaces, popping your café chair back under the table before you leave and, looking up from your mobile phone while you're out and about make a difference.

Mum says that you can also call your local council to report issues like unsafe footpaths or fallen or overgrown branches. These small actions make life much easier and safer for everyone, but most especially for a person with a vision impairment. It also makes my job easier.

Being mindful of small, everyday actions can and does make a significant difference. Small steps like moving obstacles out of the way, keeping public spaces clear of obstructions, and being aware of one's surroundings help create a more inclusive and accessible environment for everyone in our community.

Small efforts to advocate for improved accessibility and safety are truly valuable, as they greatly enhance the quality of life for those with disabilities.

####

Although I do not drive, I had an awkward experience with disability parking recently when I went shopping with my mate for some new tiles. He's renovating his house and said he wanted my opinion as I have good taste, even though I can't see the difference in colours, etc.

I jumped at going because it beats staying home and doing nothing. He parked in the only disability parking spot with my permit on display, but a car was illegally parked in the yellow-hatched area. When we were in the store, a staff member, who turned out to be the store manager, admitted it was her car, and she parks there all the time. She shrugged off our explanations of the law, which led me to make a report to the local council; their response was that I needed to discuss it with the head office of the business.

The head office responded that the area is designated for their business's customers. To my mind, this is unacceptable as the yellow shaded area is to give extra space for people with a disability the ability to get out of a car. Whether it is a motorised wheelchair, walking frame, assistance dog, etc, we need the room to safely get out of a vehicle and stop a nearby car from being dented or scratched.

Keegan and I believe that by working together, we do our bit to make our communities more understanding and welcoming.

No Excuse for Abuse!!!

Disability Discrimination Act was introduced in 1992,
After all these years, don't tell me you had no clue.

Ignorance is not above the law,
Your discrimination will be no more.

Your fear of dogs is no excuse,
And I will not allow your verbal abuse.

Having an allergy doesn't give you a right,
To refuse a guide dog and put up a fight.

The law overrides your religious objection,
So, show some respect and follow legal direction.

Guide, Hearing and Assistance Dogs Act was introduced
in 2009,
So just let us in and everything will be fine.

Refusing entry to a guide dog can result in a fine or legal
action,
And give your business negative media attraction.

Now open the door and let me through,
So I can join the queue to order some brew and good ole
Irish stew!

How to Behave Around A Guide Dog

When you meet a person with a guide, hearing, or assistance dog, it is important to remember that the dog is working. Even though it may appear that the dog is not performing a task at that moment, it is still on call and must give its full attention to the person it accompanies.

The handler's life is in the hands of the Guide Dog.

Failing to follow behaviour protocols around the handler and Guide Dog can have serious consequences.

HOW TO BEHAVE AROUND A GUIDE DOG:

• Speak to the handler first

• Do not talk to, call, or make sounds at the dog

• Do not touch the dog without asking – and receiving – permission

• Do not be offended if asked not to pat the dog

• Do not feed the dog

• Do not give commands to the dog – this is the handler's job

• Do not ask personal questions about the person's disability or intrude on their privacy

• Do not be offended if the person declines to chat about the dog

• Remember that the dog is highly trained

• Teach others that the dog is working

• Be aware that guide, hearing and assistance dogs are allowed in public places, including National Parks

AUTHORS NOTE

20 February 2024 marked 34 years since I lost my sight because of medical negligent brain surgery. I was given a maximum of 5 years to live after the medical mishap, but as my dear friend says, "Only the good die young, so you will live forever".

Life prior to Keegan was very active. I worked six days a week and socialised every day possible. Now, I only work from home. To reduce the risk of discrimination, all of my appointments are now online or over the phone. Appointments that required face-to-face interaction (physio, etc.) have been totally removed from my program.

Whilst this new lifestyle is not good for my mental health, I have adjusted to it, as discrimination, refusals, abuse and threats are certainly not good for my mental health either. In fact, it has a very serious effect on me due to my abusive history which is discussed in my previous book *'Running for My Life.'*

I don't want special treatment or exemptions; I want to be able to walk into a shopping centre, supermarket, hotel, motel, accommodation, clothing store, hairdresser, restaurant, cafe, tattoo studio, etc, without the fear of discrimination, abuse or threats.

Keegan and I should be able to enter the public venue like a parent pushing a pram, or a young man in a wheelchair, or a person of colour, or an elderly lady using a walking frame. It's not as if any customer will be told to leave their wheelchair, glasses, baby, walking frame, etc outside. Yet, although Keegan is my eyes, I am often expected to leave him outside.

Keegan is brushed every day at home to minimise dog hair shedding. He is also bathed by a mobile dog wash on a fortnightly basis, which keeps him clean and smelling fresh. A GHAD Public Access Test must be undertaken every three years, so Keegan is kept up to date with training, maintains his qualifications, and passes the Public Access Test.

My journey has not been easy, but I choose to look at the world in a positive light, use my voice to create change, and take affirmative action even when it feels like it may be easier to simply give up.

This book has been challenging to write on several levels, but it is a story that needs to be shared. We need to shine a light on discrimination and say enough is enough. Everyone deserves to be treated with kindness and respect.

I hope that between these pages, you have gleaned an insight into the world that is too often shut out and shut off from mainstream society despite a Guide Dog.

Janice Whittle
Queensland, Australia

"Keegan and Janice experience challenges every week despite her voice being heard by many, but obviously not loud enough for the next town or transport company to realise they are on the way to engage in their community and human rights enable them to do it."

Kerry Weaver
Support Coordinator & formerly at Guide Dogs Queensland

Acronyms

GHAD - Guide, Hearing & Assistance Dogs
HRC - Human Rights Commission
NDIS - National Disability Insurance Scheme
PAT - Public Access Test

www.ingramcontent.com/pod-product-compliance
Lightning Source LLC
Chambersburg PA
CBHW060931050726
47592CB00003B/900